D0765494

Freewill and responsibility

Freewill and responsibility

Anthony Kenny

Fellow of Balliol College
Oxford

Routledge & Kegan Paul
London, Henley and Boston

First published in 1978
by Routledge & Kegan Paul Ltd
39 Store Street,
London WC1E 7DD,
Broadway House,
Newtown Road,
Henley-on-Thames,
Oxon RG9 1EN and
9 Park Street,
Boston, Mass. 02108, USA
Set in 12 on 13pt Times Roman by
Computacomp (UK) Ltd, Fort William, Scotland
and printed in Great Britain by
Redwood Burn Ltd
Trowbridge and Esher

British Library Cataloguing in Publication Data

Kenny, Anthony John Patrick

Freewill and responsibility.
1. Criminal Law   2. Free will and determination
I. Title
345'.001   [Law]   78-40678

ISBN 0 7100 8998 8

Contents

Preface   vii

1   The mind and the deed   1
2   Choice and determinism   22
3   Purpose, intention and recklessness   46
4   Reason, deterrence and punishment   69

Appendix   95

Index   99

Preface

This book contains a revised version of lectures first given in 1976 as the Ryle Lectures on the Machette Foundation at Trent University, Peterborough, Ontario. I am greatly indebted to the authorities at Trent, and in particular to the Philosophy Department, for their invitation and their most friendly hospitality. Later versions of the lectures were given at Oxford and at University College London. I am indebted to members of the lecture audience on all of these occasions for their helpful comments. The lectures have now been extensively revised in the light of these comments and of recent developments in English law. I have not, however, attempted to alter the general form and style of the lectures.

The legal cases discussed in the lectures can almost all be found in Smith and Hogan's casebook, *Criminal Law : Cases and Materials* (1975). I have also learned a great deal, though no doubt not as much as I should have done, from the same learned authors' textbook, *Criminal Law* (third edition). Many years ago my interest in the philosophical aspects of criminal law was stimulated by Professor Glanville Williams's *The Mental Element in Crime*. On many occasions I have had the benefit of lively discussions with Professor H. L. A. Hart, with Professor Hans Oberdiek and with Mr J. C. McCrudden. I am particularly indebted to Dr Alan Milner of Trinity College, Oxford, who drew my attention to the African cases discussed in the first chapter and allowed me the use of his very illuminating collection of material relevant to the problems raised in criminal law by supernatural beliefs (The African Law Reports, Malawi Series, vol. 4, 1966–8, ed. Alan Milner, Oceana Publications Inc., Dobbs Ferry, New York, 1970).

The book is an attempt to apply, in the practical field of the criminal law, and in a philosophically non-technical manner, the philosophical account of human action and volition that I gave in *Action, Emotion and Will* (1963) and *Will, Freedom and Power* (1975).

Anthony Kenny
Balliol College
Oxford

29 September 1977

1   The mind and the deed

The topic of responsibility is an area in which the interests of the philosopher and of the lawyer overlap. One branch of philosophy is the philosophy of mind and action, and one of the concerns of the criminal lawyer is the mental element in crime. This area of overlap will be the subject of this book.

Philosophers of mind are concerned with the analysis of the relationship between mind and behaviour. When we understand, respond to, and evaluate each other's actions we make constant use of mentalistic concepts. On the basis of what people do, and in order to explain what they do, we attribute to them certain desires and beliefs. We ascribe their actions to choices, and we invoke, to explain their conduct, various intentions, motives and reasons. These mentalistic concepts, such as *desire*, *belief*, *intention*, *motive* and *reason*, are the subject matter of the philosophy of mind. In human action we look for a mental element; in the philosophy of human action we study the relationship between the mental element and the overt behaviour.

Actions are sometimes the subject of moral and legal evaluation: some actions we regard as admirable and praiseworthy; others we condemn and punish as criminal. Those human actions which are crimes are of special interest and have long been a subject of special study. Crimes, like other actions, involve a mental element. For this mental element lawyers have a special name: *mens rea*, which is the Latin for 'guilty mind'. There was a maxim of the English common law: *actus non facit reum nisi mens sit rea*: an act does not make a man guilty unless his mind is guilty too. The 'guilty mind' need not be any consciousness of wickedness nor any malevolent intent: in most cases it is simply a knowledge of what one is doing, where what one is doing is something illegal. But where *mens rea* is required, no act can be criminal unless accompanied by a certain mental state. The particular mental state indicated by *mens rea* differs, as we shall see, from crime to crime: the expression means, in general, the state of mind which must accompany an act which is on the face of it criminal if the agent is to be held responsible, and therefore liable for punishment, for the action.

This notion of responsibility will be the major topic of this book. The scope and method of the chapters will be philosophical in the narrow sense of the word current in Anglo-American academic circles: I shall be engaged in the analysis and clarification of certain concepts which are central to our understanding of human nature and activity. I shall not be advancing empirical hypotheses about human behaviour, nor reporting scientific discoveries about human mental processes. Nor shall I be offering an elementary course in aspects of criminal law. But I shall constantly draw upon actual legal cases to illustrate the conceptual points that I wish to make. This is not because I believe that the notions of belief, intention, choice and the like are only at home in the formal context of criminal proceedings: on the contrary, as I have said, I believe that the use of them is indispensable at every step when we endeavour to understand and communicate with each other. But the reports of the courts and the decisions of judges provide a fund of material for philosophical study which is more concrete, vivid, and credible, while at the same time often more extraordinary and thought-provoking, than any product of philosophers' imaginations. Moreover, the needs of the courts to reach a decision, and the experience of legal systems over long periods of practical operation, have in some areas brought a precision into legal concepts which can contrast favourably with the achievement of philosophers. Finally, by concentrating on legal cases in which matters of life and death are considered and in which the lifetime fate of the accused may be in the balance, we remind ourselves that the philosophy of action, while it may operate at a very abstract level, is a subject of great practical importance whose aim is to dispel confusions that can have far-reaching social consequences.

For several reasons the notion of responsibility and the cluster of concepts that combine to provide its habitat have been looked on with disfavour in recent years. To many people the apparatus of responsibility as administered in the criminal courts seems antiquated and inhumane: many social reformers look forward to a day when the courts of the criminal law have gone the way of rotten boroughs and ordeal by combat. They look forward to a time when law courts are replaced by something more scientific and clinical: when the determination of responsibility and the handing down of penalties by judicial bodies is replaced by the diagnosis of social illness and the prescription of appropriate medicinal procedures by teams of social scientists.

In these lectures I shall argue that many attacks on the common-law notion of responsibility are based on misunderstandings of an essentially philosophical nature. Conceptual confusions, I shall argue, often distort the benevolent and liberal intentions of social reformers and ensnare them into making proposals whose effects are abhorrent.

To illustrate the type of objection made by social reformers to the notions of *mens rea* and responsibility I shall quote from the evidence laid by the National Association for Mental Health before the Butler Committee which inquired into the treatment of mentally abnormal offenders and which reported in 1974. Under the heading 'The Determination of Criminal Responsibility' the Association submitted as follows:[1]

Until very recently the concept of 'mens rea' was the basis of all decisions regarding responsibility. This position was eroded by the introduction of the concept of diminished responsibility in the 1958 Homicide Act. We recognise and applaud the liberal intention behind the concept, but it is all the same a difficult one, particularly as in some cases of mental illness the diminution of responsibility may be periodic and not permanent. The position is further complicated by the fact that there are now a number of 'absolute' offences, where a person may be found guilty although he had no knowledge that what he was doing was an offence and no intention of committing an offence. Examples of such offences range from parking offences to being in possession of dangerous drugs.

The Association has considerable reservations about the present confused situation. The difficulty arises over the imprecise nature of psychiatric definition of mental disorder. This means that we constantly see the unedifying clash of psychiatric experts for the defence and the prosecution in an effort to determine the state of man's mind, when this is very often not susceptible of scientific proof. Indeed such proof would only be obtainable in the highly unlikely event of a psychiatrist observing and assessing the offender at the precise time of his offence.

We accordingly suggest for the Committee's consideration that the accused's state of mind could more profitably be taken into account in the disposal of his case than in assessing his responsibility. The disposal of cases of this kind ought to follow a very careful statement of psychiatric opinion and a full review of the social history.

Given adequate provision for taking into account a convicted person's state of mind in the decision about disposal, we suggest that the concept of '*mens rea*' and criminal responsibility could be dispensed with in favour of the concept of strict accountability for one's actions in criminal charges. We recognise, however, the radical change in sentencing procedure that would be required in this case.

The Association, therefore, wished the requirement of *mens rea* as an ingredient in crime to be replaced by a system of strict accountability for action plus a professional investigation into the accused's state of mind at the time of sentencing. In attacking *mens rea*, the Association does not seem to have had a single target in mind. It devotes itself in the paper to the consideration of when it is proper to consider an accused person's 'state of mind'. But by this expression it clearly meant several different things. Most commonly the expression is used in the paper to refer to the accused's state of mental health: Is he or she sane or insane, mentally normal or abnormal? This is naturally what the Association is most interested in and what it wants professionally investigated at the time of disposal. But in other places, by 'state of mind' the Association means such things as whether the accused knew that what he was doing was an offence and whether he had any intention of committing an offence. To investigate a state of mind in this sense is very different from inquiring into a person's state of mental health. To decide whether someone is mentally ill may well call for difficult expert inquiry by a psychiatrist – an inquiry whose difficulties would not necessarily be resolved by 'observing and assessing the offender at the precise time of his offence'. To discover whether someone knew a particular place to be a No Parking zone does not call for similar professional expertise.

The Association seems to have believed that '*mens rea*' meant knowledge that one is committing an offence, or the intention to commit an offence. This is not correct. Certainly for many crimes one needs to know that one is doing the action which is, as a matter of fact, an offence; but one does not need to know *that* it is an offence. The common law, which imposed the requirement of *mens rea*, contained also the maxim that ignorance of law was no defence. The *mens rea* which is needed for most crimes is not knowledge that X, which one is doing, is a crime; but simply the knowledge that one is doing X.

The state of mind which constitutes *mens rea* in fact varies from crime to crime. Let us suppose that the law wishes to prohibit a certain action, and let us suppose further that it gives a description of the prohibited action in terms which contain no reference to the agent's state of mind: e.g. a description such as 'being in charge of a motor vehicle' or 'entering a prohibited place'. There are many different provisos which the law can go on to make concerning what the mental state of the agent must be if his performance of the prohibited act is to constitute a crime.

(1) Let us suppose the law makes no such proviso at all, so that the act will be punishable no matter whether the accused did know or could have known that he was doing. In that case no *mens rea* will be required for the crime and it will be an 'absolute' offence, an offence of 'strict liability'.

(2) If the law does not wish it to be punishable absolutely in this manner, let us next suppose that it wishes it to be punishable whether or not the agent actually knows that he is performing the action, provided only that he could and should have known that he was. In that case the crime will be a crime of negligence. Where there is negligence, there is voluntary unawareness of the nature of one's action. The question arises. Is negligence a form of *mens rea*? Some argue that unawareness is not a state of mind and so negligence is not *mens rea*; others argue that because negligence is voluntary and culpable unawareness, the requirement of *mens rea* is present in crimes of negligence. The terminological point is perhaps not of great importance: what is important is to distinguish crimes of negligence from crimes of strict liability.

(3) If the law does not thus wish an act to be punishable when performed by an agent who is unaware that he is performing it, let us next suppose that it wishes it to be punishable whether or not the agent intends to perform it (in the sense of wanting to perform it as an end in itself or as a means to some other end), provided only that he believes or thinks it likely that he is performing it. In that case the crime will be one of recklessness: recklessness will be the *mens rea* required for the action to be punishable.

(4) If the law does not wish an action to be punishable whenever performed by an agent with this degree of awareness, it may wish it to be punishable only when

performed intentionally by an agent as an end in itself or as a means to some other end. In this case the *mens rea* required will be the act's being intentional.

(5) Finally, the law may not wish any and every intentional performance of an action to be punishable, but only in cases where the action is done with a particular intention which the law goes on to specify. In this case the *mens rea* will be the specific intent mentioned in the definition of the crime; crimes of this kind are called crimes of specific intent, and are contrasted with the crimes in the previous category which are sometimes called crimes of basic intent.

'*Mens rea*', then, may mean anything from mere negligence to a specific intention such as the intention to assist the enemy in wartime. Later, we shall have occasion to give detailed examples of types of crime in each of these five categories, and indeed on the borderlines between them. For the moment it is enough to note that as we go from the beginning to the end of this scale, the requirement of *mens rea* becomes more strict: as we go further in the scale the prosecution has to establish more and more about the accused's state of mind in order to secure conviction. The issue of soundness or unsoundness of mind is a quite separate issue, which may apply differently to different categories of crime, as we shall see later. But the general background assumption to these gradations of *mens rea* is that the accused is of sound mind: even in the cases of strict liability this is so.

The nature of strict liability is misleadingly represented in the National Association for Mental Health's submission quoted above. It is in no way a special feature of crimes of strict liability that the accused can be convicted though he has no knowledge that he is committing an offence: this is so in the great majority of crimes. Nor is it peculiar to crimes of strict liability that one can be convicted even though one did not know that one was doing the act which is, as a matter of fact, an offence: this is the case with all offences of negligence. One can, for instance, be guilty of driving without due care and attention even though at the time one did not know that one's driving was careless. The peculiar feature of absolute offences is that one can be found guilty even though one did not know, and could not reasonably have known, that one was performing the prohibited action. Selling adulterated milk and driving a motor car uninsured have been held in English law to be offences of this kind. A supplier of milk may be guilty of the former offence if milk reaches his customer in an adulterated form even though he delivered it in sound condition to a reputable carrier. If the requirement to provide third-party insurance is interpreted strictly, then I can be found guilty of driving a car uninsured if my insurers go bankrupt as I drive along the motorway.

It is not clear whether the National Association for Mental Health wishes *mens rea* to be replaced in all offences with liability that is absolute in this strict sense. If so, the proposal is surely totally unacceptable. If it were accepted, many innocent people could find themselves convicted and then – if the psychiatrists decided that it was in their or the public interest – detained against their will for indefinite periods. Suppose that I absentmindedly walk out of a bookstore with a book I have not paid for, and that as soon as I leave the store I realise what I have done and instantly go back to pay. According to the Association's proposal I would be guilty of theft, having appropriated the property of another, and evidence that I had no dishonest intent would be neither here nor there. When I had been found guilty, there would then follow 'a very careful statement of psychiatric opinion and a full review of the social history'. If the psychiatrists discovered that I had a history of odd, though not criminal, behaviour, then in accordance with a proposal of the Association not reproduced above, I would be liable to be committed to a special secure hospital.

It has been often remarked that the undesirable consequences of any proposal to abolish the requirement of *mens rea* come out particularly clearly in the case of the law of perjury. In any situation in which witnesses contradict each other on oath, one of them is making a statement which is objectively false. As things are, of course, no perjury is involved in this utterance of falsehood as long as the witness honestly believes that he is speaking the truth. But if the consideration of the accused's state of mind were to be abolished in the criminal law, then such things as his beliefs and his intentions would become irrelevant. In every clash between two witnesses one at least would be guilty of perjury and could be handed over to the psychiatrists at the Queen's pleasure forthwith.

Consider again the law of treason. English wartime defence regulations made it an offence to do an act likely to assist the enemy with intent to assist the enemy. On the reformers' proposal, of course, the mentalistic proviso, 'with intent to assist the enemy', would have to be omitted. This would no doubt have the advantage of securing rapid promotion for junior officers, as their seniors were tried for treason and removed to strict security hospitals for mistaken orders in the field. Few, indeed, at any level would be secure. During the German invasion of Greece in 1941, Churchill ordered several British North African divisions to Greece. This act, as was foreseeable, materially assisted the German war effort: it failed to prevent the conquest of Greece, and it enabled the Axis to make substantial gains in Libya and Egypt. If the question of intent were to be ruled immaterial, this order, and countless others like it, could count as treasonable.

Objections to the notion of responsibility, I have claimed, are often based on conceptual confusion. But the objections, and the confusions on which I claim they are based, are of several different kinds. The principal ones can be grouped into three classes: the epistemological, the metaphysical, and the ethical. The epistemological objection to the notion of *mens rea* stems from the idea that it is impossible, or at least impracticably difficult, to ascertain the state of mind of a man in a way sufficient to determine *mens rea*. The metaphysical one starts from a presumption that science has shown, or made it extremely likely, that determinism is true. If every act of every human being is determined in advance by inexorable laws of nature – so the objection runs – then it seems unfair to single out particular actions for judgment and reprobation. Moreover, it may well seem pointless to try to change or affect people's actions by punishments or the threat of punishments, if everything they will ever do is predictable in advance from laws and conditions that obtained before ever they were born. Finally, the ethical objection to the notion of responsibility envisages it as tied up with a theory of retributive punishment, a view of punishment as allotting to a criminal his strict deserts, rendering evil for evil, an eye for an eye and a tooth for a tooth, in a barbarously vindictive manner.

In the next chapter I will try to cut out the metaphysical root of the objection to responsibility; in chapter 4 I will try to remove the ethical root of the objection. In this chapter I will attack the epistemological root, which is the philosophical error often called by professional philosophers 'dualism'.

Dualism is the idea that mental events and states belong to a private world which is inaccessible to public observation: the belief in two separate realms of mental and physical realities which interact, if at all, only in a highly mysterious manner that transcends the normal rules of causality and evidence. The most impressive modern presentation of dualism was the philosophy of Descartes in the seventeenth century. Most contemporary philosophers reject such Cartesian dualism but its influence is great even upon those who explicitly renounce it. In extreme reaction to Cartesian ideas there grew up in the present century a school of behaviourists, who denied the existence of the mental realm altogether, maintaining that when we attribute mental states or events to people we are really making roundabout statements about their actual or hypothetical bodily behaviour. Behaviourism was for long very influential among psychologists; and among the philosophers a subtle and not quite thoroughgoing form of behaviourism was espoused in our own times by Gilbert Ryle.

The most significant philosopher of mind in the twentieth

century, however, was Ludwig Wittgenstein: and Wittgenstein thought that both dualists and behaviourists were victims of confusion. Wittgenstein's own position was a middle stance between dualism and behaviourism. Mental events and states, he believed, were neither reducible to their bodily expressions (as the behaviourists had argued) nor totally separable from them (as the dualists had concluded). According to Wittgenstein the connection between mental processes and their manifestations in behaviour is not a causal connection discoverable, like other causal connections, from the regular concomitance between the two types of events. To use Wittgenstein's technical term, the physical expression of a mental process is a *criterion* for that process: that is to say, it is part of the concept of a mental process of a particular kind (a sensation such as pain, for instance, or an emotion such as grief) that it should have a characteristic manifestation. To understand the very notion of a given mental state, one has to understand what kinds of behaviour count as evidence for its occurrence; and the relation between the behavioural evidence and the mental state is not an inductive one, not, that is to say, a connection established by the observation of the co-occurrence of two sets of independently identifiable events.

I do not intend here to expound or to defend Wittgenstein's philosophy of mind: I have tried to do elsewhere.[2] I merely observe that in so far as the epistemological objection to the notion of responsibility rests upon philosophical presuppositions, those presuppositions have in recent times been the subject of decisive criticism within philosophy itself. If Wittgenstein is right, there is no epistemological reason to reject the mentalistic concepts which are used in the legal assessment of responsibility, and no reason to think that we are setting judges and juries an impossible task in requiring them to have regard to the state of mind of an accused at the time of the commission of a criminal act. When we infer from behaviour and testimony to mental states and activities, we are not making a shaky inductive inference to events in an inaccessible realm; the very concepts of mental states have as their function to enable us to interpret and understand the conduct of human beings. The mind itself can be defined as the capacity to acquire the abilities to behave in the complicated and symbolic ways which constitute the linguistic, social, moral, cultural, economic, scientific and other characteristically human activities of men in society.[3]

The mentalistic concepts which are used in the law cannot be understood apart from their function in explaining and rendering intelligible the behaviour of human agents. But this must not be misunderstood. When we explain action in terms of desires and beliefs we are not putting forward any explanatory *theory* to account for action. It is true that desires and beliefs explain action; but the explanation is not of any causal hypothetical form. It is not as if the actions of human beings constitute a set of raw data − actions identifiable on their faces as the kinds of actions they are − for which we then seek an explanatory hypothesis. On the contrary, many human actions are not identifiable as actions of a particular kind unless they are already seen and interpreted as proceeding from a particular set of desires and beliefs. Brief reflection suffices to show this in the case of such human actions as buying and selling, promising and marrying, lying and story-telling. But it can be true also of the most basic, apparently purely physical, actions, such as killing and letting die. In legal contexts it may well be easier to identify the state of mind of the accused and of others involved than it is to decide what, in purely physical terms, they actually did.

I would like to illustrate this by a detailed consideration of an African trial: the case of *Nyuzi and Kudemera* v *Republic*, heard on appeal by the High Court of Malawi in February 1967.[4] The case demonstrates clearly that it may be easier to decide whether an accused's state of mind fulfils the requirement of *mens rea* than to decide whether his actions answer to the description of a particular *actus reus*. The case also raises a number of important and difficult conceptual points which will deserve closer attention in later chapters. I quote from the African Law Reports:

> The appellants were charged jointly in the Resident
> Magistrate's Court, Mwanza, with (a) agreeing to hold a
> trial by ordeal contrary to s.3(2) of the Witchcraft
> Ordinance (*cap*.31) and (b) directing, controlling and
> presiding at a trial by ordeal contrary to s.3(1) of the
> Ordinance.
>   The evidence revealed that the inhabitants of a certain
> village called on the first appellant, who professed to be a
> witchdoctor, to find out why the children born in the
> village were dying soon after birth. The first appellant
> agreed to hold a trial by ordeal to discover whether there
> were any witches in the village who might be responsible
> for the deaths. Sixteen people submitted themselves
> voluntarily for a test by *muabvi*, the belief being that the
> *muabvi* would kill any witches who drank it but would
> not affect the innocent. The first appellant prepared the
> *muabvi* which was handed to the 16 participants by the
> second appellant. Four of the 16 died and several others
> became ill as a result of the trial. The *muabvi* was
> submitted to a government analyst, who reported that is
> was not poisonous, and the pathologist who examined the
> deceased found no cause of death and no trace of poison
> in the bodies. The first appellant was convicted on both
> counts; the second appellant was acquitted on the first
> count but convicted on the second.
>   The first appellant appealed on the grounds that he was
> an experienced witchdoctor who, in holding the trial by
> ordeal, was performing a useful service at the villagers'
> own request, and that the deaths were caused by magic
> because the deceased were magicians. The second
> appellant appealed on the ground that he did not profess
> to be a witchdoctor and had merely acted as an assistant to
> the first appellant.

One of the issues before the Court was whether the second
appellant – the acolyte – had been rightly convicted: his

conviction was in fact varied on appeal, for reasons of no current interest. I will consider only questions which arise concerning the first appellant, Nyuzi; and I shall concentrate on three questions: Did he kill the deceased? If he did kill them, did he kill them intentionally? If he did kill them intentionally, did he murder them?

First, then, did the witchdoctor kill, or cause the deaths of the villagers who died? From several remarks in the course of his judgment it is clear that the High Court judge, Cram J., thought it correct to say that Nyuzi had killed his victims. But this must be something of a question, given what we are told in the course of the judgment:

> A government analyst examined bark and powder found in the possession of the appellant but reported that they were not poisonous; experiments on animals showed that *muabvi* was not fatal, at least to guinea pigs. The pathologist found no cause of death in the deceased, but she believed that the cause of death might be poison. She conceded, however, that she found no poison.

The judge referred to an interesting, but unsubstantiated, theory that *muabvi* while not in itself fatal to human beings becomes toxic when associated with adrenalin: so that a person frightened by the ordeal, whose glands were activated, would internally manufacture a poison. The defence case was, in a manner, parallel to this: that the deaths were the result not of Nyuzi's action but of the internal activity of the witches' magic.

Among the members of seminars and classes to whom I have described this case in England and the USA I have found that opinion is fairly evenly divided on the question, Did Nyuzi kill the deceased? Some feel strongly in favour of an affirmative answer, some feel strongly in favour of a negative answer, and some are undecided. By contrast, it is usually easy to secure unanimous agreement about the description of Nyuzi's state of mind: he intended to submit the villagers to a test which, if they were witches, would lead to their death. Here is a case, then, in which it is much easier to reach a decision about a relatively complicated form of *mens rea* than about a relatively simple type of *actus reus*.

Those of us who feel, as the judge did, that it is natural on the facts of the case to say that Nyuzi killed his victims must admit, as the judge did, that no one knows how he did it. The reason that we say, if we do, that he killed the deceased is that we know that he believed the application of the ordeal could cause the death of witches, and that he intended to apply the ordeal. The action can only be identified as a killing because we have previously identified the state of mind as a type of conditional intent to kill. It might be objected that we do not need to identify the witchdoctor's state of mind in order to regard his action as a killing: we need merely believe that he possesses mysterious powers which he exercised in this case. But this suggestion does not, in fact, escape the route through a judgment about the witchdoctor's mind: for the only reason we say – if we do – that he possesses special powers is that this kind of thing happens when he *wants* it to happen.

It was not, in fact, necessary in the case of *Nyuzi* to decide whether the accused had caused the death of the deceased, since the trial was not for murder but for violation of the law against witchcraft. The Malawi witchcraft ordinance reads, in part: 'trial by the ordeal of *muabvi* ... or by any ordeal which is likely directly or indirectly to result in the death of or bodily injury to any person shall be and is hereby prohibited.' Directing a trial by ordeal, if death results, is punishable by life imprisonment; if not, by seven years' hard labour.

No doubt it is in part at least because *muabvi* is non-toxic that witchfinders who administer it are not charged with murder: there must arguably be ground for reasonable doubt as to whether the administration of it actually causes death. In earlier times, witchdoctors offering *muabvi* have been charged and convicted of murder. One such, Palamba, had his appeal against conviction allowed by the Court of Appeal for Eastern Africa in 1947: not, however, because he

did not cause death, but because he had no intent to kill.[5]
Muabvi, the court argued, was not believed in the appellant's
culture to be poison: an additional element was needed to
cause death: the guilt of sorcery in the person who died after
taking it. But witchcraft, the court went on to say, did not
exist; therefore the deceased was innocent of witchcraft. 'On
the basis that the deceased was innocent of witchcraft, where
was malice aforethought in the appellant who, *ex hypothesi*,
believed that the administration of *muabvi* to a person
innocent of witchcraft would not cause death?'

The argument of the court in *Palamba* seems to have been
that the accused's intent can be expressed thus: I intend to
kill X if X is a witch. This is a conditional intention, not an
absolute intention. But it is a conditional the antecedent of
which is necessarily false, since there are no such things as
witches. Therefore it is a tantamount to no intent at all.

There is no doubt that, if a witchfinder has an intent to
kill, it is only a conditional intent; and conditional intention
is a difficult topic, which we shall have occasion to consider
in a different context in a later chapter in connection with the
English law of rape. But there seems to be no doubt that a
conditional intent can be a sufficient *mens rea* in murder as
in other crimes; and whether the antecedent of the
conditional is necessarily false seems to be less to the point
than whether the accused believes it to be necessarily false.
The argument of the court in *Palamba* was brushed aside by
the judge in *Nyuzi* with the words: 'This hardly takes
account of the intent to kill a guilty witch.'

'The real defence', the judge continued, 'even with intent
to kill, is self-defence or defence of the person of others.' The
trial, to repeat, was not a murder trial: but if self-defence can
provide a defence to murder, clearly it can provide one
against the lesser offence prohibited by the witchcraft
ordinance. It is well established in English and Malawi law
that defence of the person of others against a felonious attack
is as legitimate a defence in law as self-defence: but the
difficulty of admitting the defence in the present case is that
the belief in the existence of the threat which is to be warded

off depends upon the belief in witchcraft, and the question arises: Is this belief a reasonable one?

The deaths of the children complained of by the villagers were, no doubt, explicable in scientific terms, such as invasion of their bodies by a harmful organism, genetic defects, lack of care and attention or malnutrition. A person in ignorance of scientific knowledge, believing the deaths caused by sorcery, can regard the killing of the witch reputed responsible for the deaths as justified in defence of person. In this culture to destroy the witch may be considered non-culpable and even meritorious. In the light of knowledge of a modern scientific culture, he acts under a mistake of fact. Section 10 of the Penal Code (*cap.* 23) runs:
'A person who does … an act under an honest and reasonable, but mistaken, belief in the existence of any state of things is not criminally responsible for the act … to any greater extent than if the real state of things had been such as he believed to exist. …'
The kernel of the problem appears in the word 'reasonable'. To what or to whom can what is 'reasonable' be related?

The issue of the reasonableness of belief in witchcraft has been raised in a number of African cases which were murder cases, in which the death of supposed witches had been brought about not by an ordeal but by perfectly normal means. In *Jackson* the accused believed that an elderly female relation had put a spell on him, and he killed her with a bow and arrow and a hoe in the belief that this was the only way of averting his own imminent death.[6] His defence of self-defence was allowed at the trial, on the grounds that there was 'no difference in principle between a physical and a metaphysical attack'. On appeal, however, by the Attorney-General, it was held that the proper verdict should have been one of murder: the Federal Supreme Court was of the opinion that under the English common law a belief in the efficacy of witchcraft was unreasonable because it would not be accepted by the man in the street in England. This decision was queried by a number of courts before it was finally overruled in 1967 by the Supreme Court of Appeal of Malawi. As the High Court judge put it in the case of *Lufazema* which led to the overruling of *Jackson*:[7]

> Granted that the use of force in defence of person or property is governed by the principles of the English common law, does that, however, necessitate going the further step of choosing the average man in an English street? ... Surely one does no violence to the principle (that the test of reasonableness is the reaction of the man in the street) by insisting that when it is applied in Malawi, it must mean a Malawi street.

On the other hand, a court argued in a parallel case (*Ifereonwe*),[8] the mere prevalence of a belief does not make it reasonable.

> It would be a dangerous precedent to recognise that because of a superstition, which may lead to a terrible result as is disclosed by the facts of this case, is generally prevalent among a community, it is therefore reasonable.

The case with which we have been principally concerned, *Nyuzi*, was heard before *Jackson* had been overruled; but the judge did not hesitate to dissent from it, remarking that what seems reasonable according to today's science in Manchester might not be the appropriate criterion by which to judge a person whose pre-scientific beliefs had been inculcated in the bush on the banks of the Zambesi river. In the view of the pre-scientific culture in which he was steeped, the appellant was intervening to prevent felonious deaths by the evil powers of witchcraft. 'The common law requires *mens rea* as an element of a criminal offence. If a person, however, does not know the factual basis for the criminality of his act, how can he know his act is wrong?'

The judge eventually upheld the conviction, though clearly with grave misgivings about the ethical propriety of his decision. The legislature, he said, had enacted an absolute statutory liability for acts of witchcraft: 'inherent in the statute is the requirement that the actor realises what he is doing, but he need not have *mens rea*.' He concluded:

What is required is some solution which will keep this potentially dangerous person under some sort of control until he can be safely released on society, but which will also meet the ethical objection raised when a person without moral guilt is used as an example to others. It must be conceded that this kind of control simply does not exist. The only power the court has to segregate or to restrain is by imprisonment. The court must be guided as to the extent of loss of liberty by the certain risk to the community should the appellant be released in the present state of his beliefs. In all these circumstances, although a sentence of seven years' imprisonment with hard labour may offend ethical principles, it does give a practical solution to the risk to the community. Were the appellant to receive and accept some scientific explanations or to renounce his beliefs, consideration might be given in another place to a release upon licence, but not otherwise. For these reasons the appeal against conviction and sentence is dismissed.

The case was clearly a very difficult one, and the judge's manifest efforts to be fair to all concerned and his embarrassment at the apparent impossibility of doing so cannot but evoke sympathy and admiration. None the less, there is something rather puzzling both about his own account of the effect of his decision and the reasons which he gives for reaching it. The effect of the decision was to rule out self-defence as a defence to the charge of holding a trial by ordeal, and this decision was clearly necessary if the entire prohibition on ordeals was not to be nullified, since if the defence applied once it would apply always. But this does not make the offence into an absolute one: the intent to perform the prohibited action must be there, and that is the form that *mens rea* takes in the majority of crimes. Moreover, in order to rule out self-defence there is no need to make the test of a reasonable belief the reactions of an English man in the street. As was observed by the court in *Lufazema*: 'belief in the efficacy of witchcraft might have been held unreasonable for the average man in Malawi also.' If legislation is imposed with the express purpose of stamping out a system of beliefs with evil social consequences – whether it be the belief in witchcraft or the belief in the superiority of one race over another – then the belief that it is introduced to eliminate cannot be regarded as reasonable. The reference is not to English culture, or to expediency in contrast with justice, but with reference to what the Malawi legislature wished to obtain in Malawi. Assuming that the Malawi legislature was right in imposing the witchcraft statute, then a court would surely be right in holding that a belief in witchcraft was not a reasonable belief.

If there is something wrong with punishing an accused such as Nyuzi, it is surely not that he believed what he was doing to be morally right, nor that the majority of the members of his community would share his belief. The question which really imposes an objection to the enforcement of witchcraft statutes in cases such as *Nyuzi* is rather: Is it right to punish someone for an action undertaken in the light of beliefs which in his situation he could not help but have? This is a particular form of the very general question of whether it is justifiable to blame or punish a person for something he has done when he could not have done otherwise.

Whether in truth the members of communities such as Nyuzi's are in such a condition of unshakeable conviction of the truth of witchcraft is a matter of fact on which it would be impudent for one unacquainted with them to express an opinion. But the question of general principle is one of the most fundamental philosophical questions that arise concerning the criminal law, and will be the topic of the following chapter. I shall consider the question in the context of particular cases arising nearer home than Malawi, but I shall begin by considering a more general question which, if answered in one way, would make the consideration of particular cases otiose. The metaphysical objection to responsibility, as I have said, arises from the supposition of determinism. If determinism is true, and if people should not be held responsible in cases where they could not do otherwise than they have done, then it seems that no one should ever be held responsible for anything. Supposing, then, that determinism is true – and surely many intelligent and well-informed people believe that it is – how can we any longer uphold the notion of responsibility in our courts of law?

NOTES

1 The National Association for Mental Health, Evidence for Submission to the Committee on Mentally Abnormal Offenders unpublished paper, pp. 1–2.
2 In A. Kenny, *Wittgenstein*, Penguin, Harmondsworth, 1975.
3 This account of the mind is expounded in the first chapter of A. Kenny, *Will, Freedom and Power*, Blackwell, Oxford, 1975.
4 *Nyuzi and Kudemera* v *Republic*, (1966–8) African Law Reports, 249.
5 (1947), 14 E. A. C. A. 96.
6 (1923–60)A. L. R. Malawi 488.
7 High Court of Malawi, 1 May 1967.
8 West African Court of Appeal, unreported; considered in *Nyuzi and Kudemera*, *op. cit.*, p. 259.

2 Choice and determinism

Determinism is often defined as the view that every event has a cause. Neither *event* nor *cause* is as simple a notion as it looks. It is not easy to give a definition of 'event' which enables one to decide, for instance, how many events take place in a given region during a given period of time. The difficulty of giving such a definition places an obstacle to the coherent formulation of determinism; for present purposes I shall assume, without prejudice, that such difficulties can be overcome, and that among 'events', however the term is defined, will be included the movements of human bodies and the thoughts that pass through human minds. By 'cause' I will mean sufficient antecedent condition: that is to say, a state or event preceding in time the event to be explained, such that it is a sufficient condition for the occurrence of such an event. This means that there is a covering law to the effect that whenever such a causal condition obtains, it is followed by an event of the appropriate kind. So if determinism is true, it will be the case for any event E that there was an antecedent event or state C such that there is a true covering law to the effect that whenever a situation such as C obtains there will follow an event such as E. Every event will fall under a description such that there exists a law from which, in conjunction with a description of the antecedent conditions, it can be deduced that an event of that description will occur.

There are many different types of determinism answering to this very general scheme. The differences between types of determinism depend on the terms and concepts to be used in the description of the antecedent conditions and of the covering law. Indeed, it is only the possibility of specifying types of description and types of law which prevent the scheme from being vacuous as a characterisation of determinism.

One form of determinism is couched simply in terms of logical laws. Since ancient times some philosophers have thought that it could be shown by pure logic that everything is determined by inexorable fate. 'What will be, will be' is undoubtedly a logical truth: from this truth many have sought to deduce the more interesting truth that what will be must be: that whatever happens could not have happened otherwise. The purely logical arguments for fatalism are, in my view, all fallacious, though the fallacies are not always easy to pin down.

Another venerable form of determinism is theological determinism, which seeks to establish determinist conclusions from theological premises. According to theological determinism everything in the universe happens of necessity because the universe is the creature of an all-powerful and all-knowing God. Many have argued that if God knows everything from all eternity then everything must be determined from all eternity. Others have deduced determinism not from God's knowledge but from God's will and power. All the events of human history, many have believed, are not only foreknown but foreordained by God, so that even the most apparently free of human actions are the result of divine predestination.

More recently other forms of determinism have been more in the forefront of academic discussion. The determinisms now most popular are determinisms in virtue of economic or social or psychological or physiological laws. Many believe that human actions are determined by the social or economic or familial environment of individuals, in such a way that someone with a complete knowledge of the histories of individuals and societies, and a complete mastery of the laws of the appropriate disciplines, would in principle be able to forecast their futures. Among the best-known of such determinists are Marx and Freud, though it is not clear how thoroughgoing and universal they intended their determinism to be. In their writings and those of their followers it is not always clear whether every detail of the future of human history is theoretically predictable, or whether even in principle only the main lines of the development of individuals and of society can be forecast.

Though there are many different kinds of determinism, deterministic theories can be grouped for philosophical purposes into two classes: psychological and non-psychological determinisms. By 'psychological determinisms' I mean determinisms whose characteristic laws contain mentalistic terms, terms for mental events and states of mind. Non-psychological determinisms are those whose laws are statable without such terms.

Psychological determinism has been popular among philosophers of certain schools for some centuries. In its traditional form psychological determinism regards action as determined by the wants and beliefs of agents, behaviour being the outward resultant of internal motivating forces operating in the mind. Many contemporary kinds of determinism are psychological in the broad sense in which I am using the term. Economic determinism, for instance, is a form of psychological determinism to the extent that it uses mentalistic notions in the identification of its data and the formulation of its laws. Passing a dollar bill voluntarily over a counter is an economic phenomenon in a sense in which accidentally dropping a dollar bill down a drain is not: this is a distinction which can only be systematically applied in virtue of the relevant notion of '*voluntariness*', which is a mentalistic concept. Notions such as purchase, property, and the profit motive all have explicit or tacit mentalistic components. Any determinism in virtue of economic laws will, therefore, be a psychological determinism.

All psychological forms of determinism, I shall argue presently, are incoherent because they misconstrue the nature of the mental phenomena to which they explicitly or tacitly appeal in their formulation. But not all forms of determinism are psychological. Physiological determinism, for instance, understood as the view that all human activity is determined via neurophysiological states of the brain and central nervous system, does not suffer from the internal incoherence which afflicts psychological determinism. The crucial question concerning physiological determinism is not so much the internal coherence of the theory as its relationship to our experience of human freedom. If the universe is deterministic, and the body is merely a complicated machine, can there be any genuinely free action?

We can only hope to answer this question if we have a firm grasp of what it means to describe action as free. Just as there are many versions of determinism, so there are many concepts of freedom. Like the versions of determinism, the concepts of freedom can for philosophical purposes be divided into two main classes. Some analyses of freedom lay most emphasis on the notion of choice or desire, others lay most emphasis on the notion of ability or power. Some define freewill as the capacity to do what one wants, others define it as the power of alternative action. On the one account, a person does something freely if he does it *because he wants to*; on the other account he does something freely if he does it *though it is in his power not to do it*. There are convenient, if archaic, names for the two kinds of freedom: terms invented by the medieval scholastics, but surviving into later philosophers such as Hume. Freedom conceived in terms of choice or wanting is liberty of spontaneity; freedom conceived in terms of power to do otherwise is liberty of indifference.

When we ask whether determinism is compatible with freedom, is seems to make a difference which concept of freedom we take as our starting point. Those who have argued for the compatibility of freedom and determinism have commonly favoured the conception of freedom as liberty of spontaneity and have often attacked the idea of liberty of indifference as incoherent and mythical. Many of these 'compatibilists' – as we may call them – have argued that there is no clash at all between the theory that all our actions are determined, and the experience that some of our actions are the results of our choices. We are free to act as we choose – so said these compatibilists – but our actions are determined because our choices in their turn are determined. We enjoy liberty of spontaneity, but not liberty of indifference; because if everything is determined then surely we never really have the power to do otherwise than we do.

Compatibilism of this kind is, in my view, mistaken. The issue of determinism and freedom cannot be simply resolved in this way by making a distinction between liberty of spontaneity and liberty of indifference. Each of the concepts of freedom is inseparably linked with the other. The type of power to do otherwise which is necessary for freedom is the power to do otherwise if one wants to. As determinists have rightly insisted against libertarians, mere indeterminacy or randomness such as that of elementary particles in quantum jumps does not amount to anything like freewill. So liberty of indifference, rightly understood, involves liberty of spontaneity. On the other hand, it cannot be true that one has acted because one wanted to unless one had in some measure and at some point the ability to act otherwise than one did. So that liberty of spontaneity is impossible for someone who does not enjoy liberty of indifference. Liberty of spontaneity and liberty of indifference are two sides of the same guinea.

The compatibilist who is also a psychological determinist is likely to deny that explanations of actions in terms of wants implies any alternative possibility of action. For an action to be free, he will say, it is enough for it to be done because it was wanted; and for it to be done because it was wanted, it is enough that it should have been caused by the want. There is no need for there ever to have been any real possibility that the action or the want should have been other than they in fact turned out to be.

This argument rests on the view that when we say that someone did something because he wanted to, the 'because' indicates a causal relationship. According to the psychological determinist, wants and beliefs are mental states or processes which stand in causal connection with bodily movements. For this to be the case, the mental events must be capable of separate identification from the physical events: they must be, as it were, separate items in the agent's biography. Moreover, these two kinds of events must be related by a causal law. But neither of these conditions hold.

It is indeed true that every voluntary action must be an action that is in some sense wanted by the agent: if it were in no way wanted then it would not be voluntary. But an action may be voluntary without there being any mental event, distinguishable from the action itself, which precedes it or accompanies it. The choice of words when writing a letter is a voluntary act; sometimes there is a mental trying out of words in imagination, but very often there is not. In ordinary everyday conversation it would be absurd to say that each word uttered is preceded by a little mental episode which is the choice of the word. In the untypical cases where there is a mental rehearsal of the words to be chosen, the rehearsal is in its turn a voluntary action; but the rehearsal is not itself preceded by a rehearsal of the rehearsal.

The word 'want' may cover many types of things, of which it is worth while to distinguish four classes. First, there are sensual appetites such as hunger, thirst, sleepiness and sexual desire. Such wants are indeed mental processes in so far as they are sensations which have an intensity, a duration, and characteristic phenomenological features. Second, there are purposes: wants for long-term and short-term goals which are valued for their own sakes. Such purposes need not be present to one's mind whenever they are operative: an intention to become an engineer after one's course may influence one's actions without being an item of consciousness in the way that a headache or a tune hummed in the head may be. Third, there are intentions to adopt means to one's ends. These wants, like purposes, may be operative in one's conduct without occupying a place in one's stream of thought; unlike purposes they may concern things not wanted or welcomed for their own sake, perhaps even things whose prospect arouses considerable distaste, such as a visit to the dentist. Finally, there is the kind of want which is the very minimum that is necessary if an action is to be voluntary: the kind of wanting which we may call 'consent'. Something is wanted in this minimal sense if it is something which the agent chooses neither as a means nor as an end, but which would not take place were it not for the agent's pursuit of one of his purposes. I cross a neighbour's field in order to take a swim in the river; as I walk on my way I do a certain amount of damage to the grass and squash a certain number of minute organisms. In one sense, I don't *want* to damage the grass or squash the organisms: doing so is neither a purpose of mine nor a means to my ends. But I do consent to these things: I prefer to do them than to give up my purposes and the means I have chosen.

In all these cases except the first, the wants can occur – i.e. the act can be correctly explained by the want – without there being any mental event distinguishable from the action which manifests the want. The action and the explanatory want, therefore, are not the separately identifiable items of the agent's biography which they must be if the relation between them is to be a causal one.

Nor is the explanatory relation between a want and an action to be given in terms of a covering law. Wants explain actions by being – in conjunction with an appropriate set of beliefs – the agent's reasons for acting. It is the reasons for action which, according to the psychological determinist, provide the causes for action. But, as I have argued elsewhere, the laws which govern practical reasoning are of a totally different form from those which govern the operation of causes.[1]

One important difference between the explanatory power of reasons and the operation of causes is this. If there is present a perfectly adequate cause for an effect, then the effect cannot but follow: for a cause is a sufficient antecedent condition for the effect, and if an alleged cause is present and the effect does not follow, we know the cause is not a genuine one. On the other hand, there may be a perfectly adequate reason for performing an action and yet the action not ensue, without this fact casting any doubt on the adequacy of the reason.

Reasons explain actions that have been performed in the same way as practical reasoning leads to decisions about actions that are to be performed. Practical reasoning – reasoning about what to do – differs from theoretical deduction in an important way: to use a convenient technical term borrowed by philosophers from lawyers, practical reasoning is *defeasible*. That is to say, a conclusion which may be a reasonable one from a given set of premisses may cease to be a reasonable one when further premisses are added. (This is because the premisses of practical reasoning set out the goals to be achieved and the possibilities of achieving them: a decision which is reasonable in the light of a narrow set of goals may be inadequate in the light of a larger set.) Because rules of practical inference are defeasible, whereas causal laws are not, reasons cannot be regarded as causes.

In the debate between libertarians and determinists, it seems to me, the libertarians have been right to insist against the determinists that there can be no genuine freedom in the absence of the power to do otherwise. The psychological determinist denies this only because he has inadequately analysed the concept of wanting. But the libertarian, on the other hand, is wrong to think that every form of determinism must rule out the power to do otherwise. The libertarian asserts this only because he has inadequately analysed the concept of power.

What does it mean to say that we can sometimes act otherwise than we do? Clearly, acting-otherwise-than-we-do is not something that is in our power: but of course not even the most extreme libertarian asserts that it is. (Lord Russell reports a guest as saying to a millionaire 'I thought your yacht was bigger than it is.' 'No', replied the peeved host, 'My yacht is not bigger than it is.') What the libertarian means is that a person acts freely when he does X only if at the relevant time he can abstain from doing X.

When we were examining the determinist case, we were

drawn to distinguish between four senses of 'want': in examining the libertarian case we must distinguish four senses of 'can'. There are four different types of thing we may be attributing when we say of someone or something that he or it *can* do such-and such. Firstly, there are natural powers such as the power of water to freeze. When the conditions are right for the exercise of a natural power, the power will inevitably be exercised: necessary conditions here are also sufficient conditions. This type of power is the determinist's paradigm, to which he attempts to reduce all other types. Secondly, there are abilities, such as a dog's ability to retrieve or a human being's ability to swim, paint, or do long division. These differ from natural powers: no matter how propitious the external conditions, an agent may on occasion refrain from exercising an ability because he does not wish to exercise it. Third, there are opportunities for the exercise of abilities. I may have the ability to swim, but in another sense of 'can' I cannot swim if there is no water around. Fourth, there is the overall sense of 'can' in which it indicates the presence of both ability and opportunity. This is the kind of power which is under discussion when freewill is said to involve the power to do otherwise.

In order to do X freely one must have both the ability and the opportunity not to do X. Now abilities are things that are inherently general: any genuine ability must be capable of exercise on more than one occasion. Even if an ability is of a kind that can be exercised only once, or even if no more than one opportunity arises for its exercise, it must always be conceivable that it should have been exercised on some occasion other than the one on which it is in fact exercised. This point is important when we are considering the ability to do otherwise which is part of the power necessary for freedom. Again, an opportunity is something which is external to an agent: if the only thing which stops you from doing something is the fact that you don't want to do it, you cannot say that you have no opportunity to do it. This point, too, is important in the context of the debate between libertarians and determinists.

Bearing these two points in mind, we can return to the question whether freedom is compatible with determinism. We have agreed that freedom involves the power to do otherwise: I do X freely only if I have the opportunity not to do X and the ability not to do X. Can this power ever be present if, say, physiological determinism is true? Can I have the ability and opportunity not to do X if I am in a physiological state from which, in conjunction with physiological laws, it can be deduced that my body will move in such a way that I will do X?

The answer, it seems to me, is that I can.

Consider first ability. Whether or not I have a given ability is settled by whether I fulfil the criteria for possessing that ability: that is to say, by whether I succeed in exercising it when I want to exercise it and when there is an opportunity for exercising it. Because abilities are inherently genuine, in order for me to fulfil these criteria on a particular occasion there is no need for me actually to exercise the ability on that occasion. And provided these criteria are fulfilled, it matters not what my current physiological state may be.

What of opportunity? Clearly, I may often have an opportunity to, e.g., strangle my kitten even though I may not on that occasion, or on any other occasion, take the opportunity. But if I am in a physical position to strangle my kitten, but my current physiological state is such that I will not strangle him, can I really be said to have an opportuinty to strangle him? Yes, indeed: there is nothing external to me preventing me. But, it might be argued, though there is nothing external to my body preventing me, is there not something external to my will preventing me, namely, the state of my brain and central nervous system? And if that is the case, surely the truth of physiological determinism would rule out the opportunity, and therefore the power, to strangle the kitten, and in general, to act otherwise than I do.

This objection does not succeed, and it is important to see why. Physiological determinism need in no way involve the theory that wants do not affect actions: if it did, it could be excluded straight off as entailing an obvious falsehood. Any plausible physiological determinism must make room for such facts as that if I wanted to strangle the kitten I would. It follows that whatever story the physiological determinist tells about my present physiological state must contain a proviso that my brain state would be different from what it now is if I wanted something different from what I now want (if, for instance, I wanted to strangle the kitten). Consequently, whatever my present state is, it is not a state such that if I wanted to strangle the kitten I could not. But only such a state would prevent me from strangling the kitten, or deprive me of an opportunity to strangle the kitten.

Physiological determinism, then, seems to leave room for both the ability and the opportunity to do otherwise than we do, and thus to be compatible with freedom, understood as liberty of indifference. But if – as this type of physiological determinism demands – every difference between wants is accompanied by a difference in physiological state, will not physiological determinism collapse into psychological determinism, which we have already rejected? No: physiological determinism would entail psychological determinism only if physiological events of a particular kind were correlated in a regular and law-like manner with psychological conditions of a particular kind. But there is no reason to believe that physiological determinism must involve such regular correlations. It may be, for all we know, that for each individual case in which a human being can choose whether to do X or not to do X there is *a* difference between the state of the brain and of the central nervous system which goes with wanting to do X, and the state which goes with not wanting to do X; and this could well be the case without there being any general laws linking physiological states of a particular kind with psychological states of a particular kind. If this is so, there is no reason why physiological determinism should lead to psychological determinism, or why predictability at a physiological level should involve predictability at a psychological level.

I have been defending the theory that the freedom of the

will is compatible with one kind of determinism. This theory, as I have observed, is sometimes called 'compatibilism': it is contrasted with the incompatibilism which regards freedom and determinism as irreconcilable. Sometimes compatibilism is identified with a philosophical theory which has been nicknamed 'soft determinism': but in reality the two positions are distinct. Soft determinism is a version of determinism: the soft determinist does believe that every event has a cause in the sense of a sufficient antecedent condition. He is called 'soft' because he believes in addition that determinism does not exclude freedom: he is contrasted with the hard determinist who thinks that determinism is incompatible with freedom and that since determinism is true freedom must be an illusion. All soft determinists are compatibilists, but the converse is not true.

Though I have defended compatibilism, I am agnostic on the issue of determinism. I know of no convincing reason for believing universal determinism to be true, and no convincing reason for believing it to be false. I do not even know whether it can be given a totally coherent formulation. Most people who have a firm belief in determinism or indeterminism seem to me to base their conviction on an act of faith, or at best on an extrapolation from the history of science. But extrapolation from the history of science may incline one to determinism or to indeterminism in accordance with the particular science, or the particular period of history, from which one decides to extrapolate.

No doubt the commonest reason for believing in indeterminism is belief in incompatibilism. Since we know we are free agents, anyone who believes that freedom is incompatible with determinism is bound to conclude to indeterminism. But if compatibilism is defensible, there is no inference from freedom to indeterminism. The issue of compatibilism is a strictly philosophical issue: it is a question about the logical relationship between two sets of concepts. But on the assumption that determinism can be coherently formulated, the issue between determinists and indeterminists is not a purely philosophical question. The question concerns the nature of the system of laws governing the universe: if this question can be answered it cannot be answered by the philosopher alone. It is an issue on which the philosopher, as such, can and should remain agnostic.

We may sum up the upshot of the discussion of determinism as follows. If compatibilism is correct, then the issue of determinism is irrelevant to the question of responsibility. The bogey of determinism cannot be used as an argument against the ascription and assessment of responsibility. For determinism might very well be true without that fact giving any reason to call in question the concept of responsibility. Still less can the concept of responsibility be undermined by the mere invocation of the possibility of determinism when, as is the case, no one really knows whether it is true or not.

Undoubtedly it is unjust to hold responsible for their actions those who lack the relevant freedom, those who could not have done otherwise than they did. But if our argument so far has been correct it does not follow from determinism that agents always lack the opportunity and ability to do otherwise than they do. Consequently it does not follow from determinism that it is unfair to hold people responsible for their actions.

We need, therefore, pay no further attention to the general metaphysical grounds for suspicion of the notion of responsibility. For the remainder of this chapter I wish to consider the way in which the legal system applies in cases in which, for particular concrete reasons, an agent lacks the power to do otherwise than perform an *actus reus*.

It is unjust to hold individuals criminally responsible for their acts and omissions unless those acts and omissions are themselves voluntary or are the foreseeable consequences of other voluntary acts and omissions. This principle is in general accepted in the criminal law, with some exceptions which we shall later consider. In a murder case, for instance, the Crown must prove that death was the result of a voluntary act of the accused. As Lord Denning put it in a famous murder case (*Bratty* v *Attorney-General for Northern Ireland*):[2] 'The requirement that it should be a voluntary act is essential, not only in a murder case, but also in every criminal case. No act is punishable if it is done involuntarily.' He went on to explain that an involuntary action was a reflex or unconscious action: an action was not necessarily involuntary because it was unintentional or unforeseen or later forgotten. To convict a person of what on the face of it is an *actus reus* the jury must be satisfied beyond reasonable doubt that the act was a voluntary one.

The question of voluntariness may be raised not only in the case of automatic or unconscious actions, but also in the case of compulsion, duress, and mental disorder. If one stronger than I takes my hand and forces it to close on the trigger of a gun then I do not pull the trigger voluntarily. No court would find me guilty on the basis of such an action, and it might be queried whether it was an action of mine at all. But the *actus reus* of a crime may be not an action but a state or condition and courts have not always found it a defence to being in a prohibited condition that one was brought into that condition by main force. In the case of *Larsonneur*[3] the accused was a French citizen who left the UK for Ireland on the day her residence permit expired. She was deported from Ireland and landed at Holyhead in the custody of the Irish police. She was then charged and convicted of the offence of being found in the UK while being an alien to whom leave to land in the UK had been refused. The verdict was confirmed by the Court of Appeal but has since been almost universally condemned: she should surely not have been held responsible for a state of affairs which she had neither voluntarily brought about nor had any opportunity to terminate.

In everyday language people are often said to be compelled to do things when no actual force is used but the actions are performed to avert the threat of violent action or imminent disaster. These are cases where it will be natural for the agent to say that he 'had no choice' but to do the prohibited action: but in fact the action is a voluntary one,

arising out of a choice between evils. When the choice
between evils is posed as a result of the wrongful threats of
another, lawyers speak of 'duress'; when it arises through
the operation of natural causes, they prefer to speak of
'necessity'.

It has long been accepted in English law that the existence
of a threat of death or extreme personal violence provides a
defence in the great majority of criminal offences.
Commonly, it has been held that duress is no defence to
murder: a man ought rather to die himself than escape
through the death of an innocent. But the issue has recently
been put to the test as the result of events in Northern
Ireland. In *Lynch* v *D.P.P. for Northern Ireland* (1975)[4] the
appellant was forced by IRA gunmen to drive them to and
from a place where they shot a policeman. The appellant,
who clearly believed that he would have been shot had he
refused to obey, had been convicted at trial of murder and
his appeal was dismissed by the Court of Criminal Appeal.
The House of Lords, by a majority of three to two, allowed
the appeal, establishing the rule that at least in cases where
the accused was not the actual killer or principal in the first
degree, duress could be a defence to murder.

A year later a further case before the Privy Council
decided that the defence of duress in murder was not
available to a principal in the first degree who did the actual
killing. In *Abbott* v *the Queen*[5] the defendant had taken an
active part in killing a woman at the command of the head of
the commune where he lived, threats having been made to
his own and his mother's life. The judgment of the court
was by a majority of three to two, the minority judges
having been two of the majority in *Lynch*. It was now
argued that even in *Lynch* a majority of the House had been
of opinion that duress was not a defence to an actual killer:
but many of the arguments of the majority in *Abbott* could
well have told against the *Lynch* decision also. To allow
duress as a defence to killers, Lord Salmon said, might prove
to be a charter for terrorists, gang-leaders and kidnappers.

A terrorist of notorious violence might e.g. threaten death
to A and his family unless A obeys his instructions to put
a bomb with a time fuse set by A in a certain aircraft,
and/or in a thronged market, railway station or the like.
A, under duress, obeys his instructions and as a result,
hundreds of men, women and children are killed or
mangled. Should the contentions made on behalf of the
appellant be correct, A would have a complete defence,
and, if charged, would be bound to be acquitted and set at
liberty. Having now gained some real experience and
expertise, he might again be approached by the terrorist
who would make the same threats and exercise the same
duress under which A would then give a repeat
performance killing even more men, women and
children. Is there any limit to the number of people you
may kill to save your own life and that of your family?

Many were disquieted by the decision in *Lynch*. The
majority judges' view that 'a law which requires innocent
victims of terrorist threats to be tried for murder and
convicted as murderers is an unjust law' naturally
commands sympathy: but it is arguable that the decision
was likely to increase, rather than diminish, the overall
sufferings of innocent victims of terrorists. For to the extent
that duress is a defence in murder, a terrorist can by threat
confer impunity on those whom he employs to further his
murderous ends.

This objection to allowing duress as a defence does not
apply to allowing as a defence necessity which arises from
natural causes. Necessity is commonly said not to be a
defence in murder: the classic case is the 1884 *R v Dudley
and Stephens*.[6] In this case two shipwrecked mariners killed
and ate a cabin boy to save themselves from starving to
death in an open boat. The defence of necessity offered by
the accused was not allowed: they were sentenced to death
for murder, though the sentence was later commuted to a
brief imprisonment.

Nowadays lawyers can be found to argue that the verdict

in *Dudley and Stephens* was too harsh and the moral principles on which it was based unacceptable: nobody can be morally obliged to be a hero, and the principle that one should never intentionally take innocent life is too rigid.[7] To me the decision in the case seems ethically sound (as does the decision to mitigate the sentence). While most people most of the time can steer a middle course between wickedness and heroism, the human condition is such that in tragic circumstances a man can be faced with a stark choice between the two. The principle that one should never intentionally take innocent life would be contested by supporters of euthanasia, who see nothing wrong with taking the life of a consenting victim. The decision in *Dudley and Stephens* can be justified by the narrower principle that one should not take innocent life in order to save one's own life. This principle seems to me, as it did to Lord Coleridge in 1884, to be correct: it seems likely to reduce the overall number of innocent deaths. Certainly I would rather be in an open boat with companions who accepted the principle than in company with lawyers who accepted necessity as a defence to murder.

The moral objection to necessity as a defence applies equally to duress. *Dudley and Stephens*, it seems, is still authoritative in law. There seems something paradoxical in a state of law which refuses necessity as a defence to murder, but which allows duress even though all the objections to allowing necessity apply equally to allowing duress, while the allowance of duress is open to the further objection that it puts a premium on murderous threats.

Whatever be the truth of this matter, it is clear that the allowance of necessity and duress cannot be argued for on the grounds that actions done under these compulsions are not voluntary actions. 'In both sets of circumstances', in the words of Lord Simon of Glaisdale,[8] 'there is power of choice between two alternatives; but one of those alternatives is so disagreeable that even serious infraction of the criminal law seems preferable. In both the consequence of the act is intended, within any permissible definition of intention.'

Clearly, in a case of duress the desire for self-preservation may well be so strong as to outweigh the desire to avoid incurring any penalties imposed by the criminal law. This sets a problem, quite distinct from the problem of the voluntariness of the action under compulsion, to which we must later return. But in the present context, we may ask whether a desire, such as the desire for self-preservation, can be so strong as literally to take away the agent's power to act in any way other than in execution of the desire. This is a problem which has been posed in legal contexts in the terms: can there be an irresistible impulse to commit a criminal action, and if so does it provide a defence?

For some reason which is unclear, those who believe in the possibility of irresistible impulses regard them as indications of insanity. The M'Naghten rules, which since they were drawn up by the judges in 1843 have governed the use of the defence of insanity in English law, state that to establish the defence it must be proved that the accused while performing the criminal act 'was labouring under such a defect of reason, from disease of the mind, as not to know the nature and quality of the act he was doing, or, if he did know it, that he did not know he was doing what was wrong.' It has often been objected to these rules that they are stated in exclusively cognitive terms: they allow for defects of knowledge, but not for defects of the emotions or the will. A prisoner should not be held responsible, the Atkin committee recommended in 1923, 'when the act is committed under an impulse which the prisoner was by mental disease in substance deprived of any power to resist'.[9]

The Royal Commission on Capital Punishment in 1953 was particularly critical of the M'Naghten rules.[10]

The charge against the M'Naghten rules is that they are not in harmony with modern medical science, which, as we have seen, is reluctant to divide the mind into separate compartments – the intellect, the emotions and the will – but looks at it as a whole and considers that insanity

distorts and impairs the action of the mind as a whole. ...
To abstract particular mental faculties, and to lay it down
that unless these particular faculties are destroyed or
gravely impaired, an accused person, whatever the nature
of his mental disease, must be held to be criminally
responsible, is dangerous.

The Commission concluded that the law on the insanity
defence should be changed, but it disliked the proposal that
the rules should be revised to include cases where irresistible
impulse was in operation. It preferred the addition of a
clause suggested by the British Medical Association to the
effect that it should be a defence to a mentally diseased
person that owing to a disorder of emotion he did not
possess sufficient power to prevent himself from committing
an act that he knew was wrong. It thought it would be even
more preferable to abolish any test such as the Rules and
leave it to the jury to determine whether the accused when
he acted was mentally diseased 'to such a degree that he
ought not to be held responsible'. It gave no clear guidance
as to the criteria it thought the jury should use to reach this
decision.

The same vagueness, not unexpectedly, is to be found in
the Homicide Act of 1957 which gave partial effect to the
proposals of the Royal Commission. The Act did not
abrogate the M'Naghten Rules, but it introduced a defence
of diminished responsibility which entitled an accused in a
murder case to be convicted instead of the lesser crime of
manslaughter. The defence is to be allowed if the jury find
that the accused 'was suffering from such abnormality
of mind ... as substantially impaired his mental responsibility
for his acts and omissions in doing or being a party to the
killing.' The defence is a curious one, since the question
whether someone is to be held responsible for his acts is a
legal or moral one, not a question of fact: the Act seems to
entrust the fate of the accused, when this defence is led, to
the moral intuitions of the jurors. Rightly or wrongly, judges
in cases under the Act have offered jurors assistance in

arriving at their intuitions. In *Byrne*[11] the accused had
strangled a young woman in a YMCA hostel and mutilated
her body in a horrifying manner. Medical evidence was
given that he had long suffered from violent perverted sexual
desires which he found it difficult or impossible to control.
The trial judge directed the jury that the medical evidence
did not amount to a defence under the relevant section of the
act, and the accused was convicted. The Court of Appeal
held that there had been a misdirection: inability to exercise
willpower to control physical acts due to abnormality of
mind was sufficient to entitle the accused to a defence.
'Thus', say Smith and Hogan in their textbook *Criminal
Law*, 'the defence of irresistible impulse is at last admitted
into the law.'[12]

In the course of the Appeal judgment in *Byrne*, the Lord
Chief Justice observed:

> In a case where abnormality of mind is one which affects
> the accused's self-control, the step between 'he did not
> resist his impulse' and 'he could not resist his impulse' is,
> as the evidence in this case shows, one which is incapable
> of scientific proof. *A fortiori*, there is no scientific
> measurement of the degree of difficulty which an
> abnormal person finds in controlling his impulses. These
> problems, which in the present state of medical
> knowledge are scientifically insoluble, the jury can only
> approach in a broad, common-sense way.

The recent Butler Committee, like the Royal Commission
before it, is critical of the notion of irresistible impulse.[13]
How, it asks, can one tell the difference between an impulse
which is irresistible and one which is merely not resisted?
The American Model Penal Code had suggested that it
should be a defence if the agent 'lacked substantial capacity
to conform his conduct to the requirement of law.' The
Butler Committee objected to this that in most cases in
practice 'it is fair to say that the only evidence of incapacity
to conform with the law is the act itself'.

The difficulty which the Butler Committee and the judgment in *Byrne* mention is indeed not an accidental and temporary one which progress in scientific knowledge and measurement techniques may in due course remove. It is an insoluble one arising from the nature of the concepts involved. If someone succumbs to the temptation of committing a criminal act there is no way even in principle of deciding whether he is a man of normal strength of will who is giving way to impulses which are stronger than normal, or is a man of unusual weakness of will giving way to normal impulses. If evidence is given to show that on many other occasions he has indulged in criminal behaviour, this may be taken with equal justice as evidence of chronically imperious impulses, or of chronic unwillingness to exercise self-control. If, on the other hand, evidence is given to show that this is a wholly uncharacteristic lapse in a life of otherwise unblemished rectitude, this in its turn may be taken with equal justice as evidence of impulses no stronger than normal, or of a degree of self-control well beyond *l'homme moyen sensuel.* Where the same behavioural evidence can be taken with equal justice as evidence for contrary mental phenomena, it is clear that the alleged mental phenomena are metaphysical fictions. In the present case, the notion of the strength of an impulse, considered as something ascertainable independently of action upon that impulse, is a fictional parameter begotten of conceptual confusion.

If an impulse is supposed to be a kind of want, then there is something self-contradictory in the notion of an irresistible impulse. Wants are attributed to people on the basis of what they do when it is open to them to do otherwise. If someone acts under irresistible pressure, then his act is not a voluntary act and therefore not an act performed because of a want. To introduce a defence of irresistible impulse is to allow that an action can be both voluntary (because performed on the basis of a want) and non-voluntary (because performed under irresistible pressure).

It may be argued that however incoherent the

terminology of irresistible impulse, it is undoubtedly possible that mental disorder may take away voluntary control, and that in such a case a defence must be available to the accused. It is indeed perfectly conceivable that actions which are within the voluntary control of normal people may, as a result of mental abnormality, cease to be subject to such control. But if they do cease to be subject to voluntary control, that means that they will be performed no matter how much it is in the agent's interest not to perform them. For to say that an action is subject to voluntary control means that it results from the agent's assessment of the attractiveness of the prospect of the action and its consequences in comparison with the other alternatives open to him. If he persists in performing the action no matter what its consequences and no matter what the other alternatives – as may be the case, say, in extreme addiction – then the action is no longer subject to voluntary control.

It follows from this, however, that the question whether an action is subject to voluntary control cannot be separated from the question of what sanctions the law provides against the commission of such an action. The point was put crudely but succinctly by a Canadian judge: 'If you cannot resist an impulse in any other way, we will hang a rope in front of your eyes, and perhaps that will help.'[14] The Royal Commission on Capital Punishment held it to be a defect in the M'Naghten Rules that even if strengthened with the provision of a defence in the case where the accused could not prevent himself from committing the criminal act, they were capable of interpretation in such a way that 'a defence of insanity on the ground that the accused was incapable of preventing himself from committing the crime was bound to fail unless the jury were satisfied that he would not have refrained from committing it even if a policeman had been standing beside him.' The members of the Royal Commission may have been more compassionate than the judges who drew up the Rules, but they were considerably less clear-headed. Incapacity to control one's action can only consistently be admitted as a defence in cases in which, even if it were not admitted as a defence, the accused would none the less have committed the criminal action: and the difficulty of proving the truth of such a counterfactual goes far to nullify its value as a defence.

Those who object to the compartmentalisation of intellect, will and emotion are themselves often the victims of the false idea which they criticise: they accept the picture of the mind as a quasi-physical apparatus with spatial parts, and merely insist that all of the spatial parts must be taken into consideration when assessing responsibility. But in fact if the intellect, will, and emotions are 'abstractions', so, in exactly the same sense, is the mind itself. The concrete, observable entities are human beings behaving in certain ways: the mind and its faculties are the capacities which manifest themselves in behaviour which is analysable in cognitive and affective terms. Precisely because the intellect and the will are not separate compartments it is rash to conclude that a set of criteria like the M'Naghten rules, which are framed in cognitive terms, automatically fail to capture the volitional dimension. The will is the capacity to behave in pursuit of long-term goals and in the light of the comparative attractiveness of alternative courses of action: because of this, an investigation of an agent's ability to understand what he is doing and its relevance to long-term goals, and of his judgments of comparative value, is not something distinct from, and irrelevant to, an inquiry into the effectiveness of his will.

All of this is not, of course, meant to suggest that the question of mental disease and disorder is irrelevant to the assessment of criminal responsibility. The conclusion to be drawn is that mental abnormality is not best considered as a condition of incapacity parallel to physical disability or compulsion by main force. It is properly to be considered in the context in which the nineteenth-century judges considered it, in its implications for the presence or absence of the *mens rea* for particular crimes. To the detailed consideration of the different forms of *mens rea* the next chapter will be devoted.

NOTES

1   The arguments summarily presented in this chapter are developed at greater length in A. Kenny, *Will, Freedom and Power*, Blackwell, Oxford, 1975, chs VI-VIII.

2   [1963] A.C. 386.

3   [1933] 149 L.T. 542.

4   [1975] 1 All E.R. 913.

5   [1976] 3 All E.R. 140.

6   [1881–5] All E.R. Rep. 61.

7   Rupert Cross, 'Necessity Knows No Law', 1968 Turner Memorial Lecture, University of Tasmania.

8   In his minority judgment in *Lynch*.

9   Quoted by J. C. Smith and B. Hogan, *Criminal Law*, 3rd edn, Butterworth, 1973, p. 139.

10   *Report of the Royal Commission on Capital Punishment*, Cmd 8932, 1953, section 324.

11   [1960] 3 All E.R. 1.

12   Smith and Hogan, *op. cit.*, p. 146.

13   *Report of the Committee on Mentally Abnormal Offenders* (Butler Committee), Cmd 6244, 1975, ch. 18

14   Quoted in Smith and Hogan, *op. cit.*, p. 139.

3 Purpose, intention and recklessness

Mens rea, as was explained in chapter 1, is the state of mind which must be present in an accused if his overt action is to constitute a crime, and if he is to be held responsible for it. This general notion fits different crimes in different ways. Criminal laws differ not only in respect of the overt actions they forbid (as murder differs from rape) but also in respect of the state of mind which they require if the action is to constitute the offence in question (as murder differs from manslaughter).

In general, an inquiry into the *mens rea* of an accused is an inquiry into his reasons for acting as he did. When we say that someone acted for a certain reason, we are attributing to him both a cognitive and an affective state: a desire for a certain state of affairs to be brought about, and a belief that a certain manner of acting is a way of bringing about that state of affairs. Cognitive states of mind are those which involve a person's possession of a piece of information (true or, as the case may be, false): such things as belief, awareness, expectation, certainty, knowledge. Affective states of mind are neither true nor false but consist in an attitude of pursuit or avoidance: such things as purpose, intention, desire, volition. Some mental states, of course, are both affective and cognitive: hope and fear, for instance, involve both an expectation of a prospective state of affairs and a judgment of the state of affairs as good or evil. Very various cognitive and affective states may constitute *mens rea* in different crimes and in different circumstances.

To justify the legal apparatus of *mens rea* and responsibility, therefore, it does not suffice to defend the general practice of inquiring into the mental state of the accused: it is necessary to investigate and evaluate the way in which in detail the law requires judges and juries to inquire into particular states of mind in particular crimes. In this chapter I wish to illustrate how in fact the law works in this respect: I will not in general try to justify or criticise these workings, but merely to elucidate them and remove some misconceptions of their nature.

The first step in such an elucidation is to separate out and characterise the various cognitional and volitional states involved, such as purpose, motive, intention, foresight, voluntariness, negligence, recklessness.

It is convenient to start with purpose. By 'purpose' we may mean a person's goal in a course of action: we may contrast the purposes which a man pursues with the means he chooses for achieving his goals, and the consequences of his actions which, though he may accept them, are no part of the task he sets himself to achieve. Purpose, so understood, is a particular kind of intention: the ultimate intention of a particular course of action.

Though the law often interests itself in people's intentions, it is rarely concerned with whether a particular intention is an ultimate intention or not. Few statutes, indeed, make use of the word 'purpose'. An exception is the English Official Secrets Act of 1911. This made it a felony to enter a prohibited place 'for a purpose prejudicial to the safety or interests of the state'. In *Chandler* v. D.P.P.[1] the appellants, who were campaigners for nuclear disarmament, had been convicted of conspiracy to commit a breach of this Act because they had tried to enter an air-base to immobilise bomber aircraft. They claimed that it would be for the benefit of the country to give up nuclear armaments, and that therefore their purpose of promoting disarmament, far from being prejudicial to the safety of the state, was in its true interest. An appeal was taken to the House of Lords, but was dismissed. The word 'purpose' in the Act, it was held, could not be taken to mean only the main object which a man wants to hope or achieve. Lord Devlin said:

Its use in that sense would make this statute quite inept. As my noble and learned friend Lord Reid pointed out during the argument, a spy could secure an acquittal by satisfying the jury that his purpose was to make money for himself, a purpose not in itself prejudicial to the state, and that he was indifferent to all the other consequences of his acts.

Lords Devlin and Radcliffe both thought that the appellants' ultimate aim was better called their 'motive'; and motive, they said, was commonly irrelevant in criminal law.

In ordinary language 'purpose' 'motive' and 'intention' often appear interchangeable. When a person does X in order to bring about Y, the prospect of bringing about Y is his reason for acting: but the reason may be pictured as something behind him pushing him on, or something in front of him presenting a target. The word 'motive' seems more appropriate for the reason viewed in the first way, the word 'purpose' for the reason viewed in the second way. 'Intention' is the most general word in use in cases in which an agent is doing one thing for the sake of another or in order to bring about another. A person intends both those things that he does or pursues as ends in themselves, and those things that he does as means to his ends. With some artificiality, we can make a gain in clarity by following the accused in *Chandler* and using 'purpose' only for ultimate intentions, goals sought for their own sake. (In ordinary language it is natural to use 'purpose' also for intermediate goals and for means which are welcomed for their own sake as well as for their value in promoting distinct goals.)

If we use 'purpose' in this sense, are a man's purposes relevant in criminal law? They are, or may be, relevant in the sense that the law often inquires into the further intentions with which a man performs a prohibited act, and if these further intentions are the man's ultimate intentions, then they are his purposes even in this artificially narrow sense. But for reasons similar to those given by Lords Reid and Devlin in *Chandler*, it will never be relevant whether that further intention is in fact an ultimate intention or purpose. Motives, then, in so far as they are equivalent to purposes, are in one sense irrelevant at law. However, lawyers often use 'motive' to mean simply 'intention with which the law does not concern itself'. Thus, if a man breaks into a house to steal money to buy medicine for his wife, he has an intent to steal, but his motive is to buy medicine. For theft is forbidden by law, but not the purchase of medicine. In this sense, of course, it becomes true by definition that motives are irrelevant in law.

The decision in *Chandler* that it does not matter what a person's ultimate intentions may be reflects the main body of legal tradition. But there is one case which suggests a contrary doctrine: that of *R* v *Steane* in 1947.[2] Steane, interned in Germany during the Second World War, had broadcast propaganda for the Nazis under threats to himself and family. He was convicted under the Defence Regulations of doing an act likely to assist the enemy with intent to assist the enemy. His conviction was set aside on the grounds that the jury should have been told that the guilty intent was not proved 'if the circumstances showed that the act was done in subjection to the power of the enemy or was as equally consistent with an innocent intent as with a criminal intent, e.g. a desire to save his wife and children from a concentration camp.

Steane's ultimate intent or purpose was undoubtedly the innocent one of saving his family: but it is hard to follow the argument of the Court of Criminal Appeal that he did not intend to assist the enemy. Helping the Germans in the way they demanded – by broadcasting – was precisely the means which, however reluctantly, he chose in order to safeguard his family. The Court was right to argue that the intent should not be presumed, in these circumstances, merely because the act was one likely to assist the enemy, and a man is taken to intend the natural consequences of his acts. In this case, the assistance to the enemy was not merely foreseen but chosen as a means to an end. If Steane was rightly acquitted on the grounds that he lacked the requisite intent, then 'intent' in the Defence Regulations must mean ultimate intent. But it is hard to resist the conclusion that it would have been better to acquit Steane on the grounds that he was subject to duress, rather than because he lacked the intent to assist the enemy.

There are a number of crimes in which – as under the Defence Regulations under which Steane was tried – the offence is not committed unless the prohibited action is done with a particular intention which is specified in the crime. Thus, forgery involves an intent to defraud, and theft involves an intention to deprive the owner permanently of his property. Here the further intention is a necessary part of the *mens rea* for the crime. Crimes of this kind are called crimes of specific intent: they are contrasted with crimes of basic intent, where there is required for *mens rea* only the intention to perform the *actus reus* of the crime. Thus, assault is an act causing another to apprehend immediate and unlawful personal violence: the *mens rea* for assault is simply the intent to perform such an act.[3]

As has been observed above, a person intends the ends he sets himself and the means he chooses to achieve those ends. In law, he intends *at least* this much: but in many contexts lawyers give the word 'intent' a wider interpretation, so that a man is taken to intend the foreseen consequences of his actions. Outside legal contexts it is not usually natural to speak of someone as intending foreseen consequences of his action when these are unwanted or when he is merely indifferent to them. I know that whenever I walk along a paved street I am very likely to tread on the boundaries between paving stones: but since I passed the age of Christopher Robin I have hardly ever either intended to step on those boundaries or intended not to step on them. Many people drink too much knowing that they will suffer a hangover, and eat too much knowing that they will put on weight: but they don't drink *in order to* produce a hangover or eat with the intention of putting on weight.

The natural concept of intention is that one intends to do what one does for its own sake, or what one does in order to some further end. This natural concept is also for theoretical purposes, in my view, the most useful. But some philosophers and many lawyers accept the view that all foreseen consequences of one's voluntary actions are intentional, whether or not aimed at as ends or means. One such philosopher was Jeremy Bentham, the eighteenth-century author of the celebrated *Principles of Morals and Legislation*. If such a view is not to be a source of confusion one must go on, as Bentham did, to draw a distinction between direct and oblique intention: oblique intention being mere foresight of consequences, and direct intention being the case where the consequences are not just a foreseen outcome but something which the agent sets out to achieve as a means or an end, and which constituted at least part of his reason for acting as he did.

Oblique intention is primarily a cognitive state: it concerns what a person knows or believes. Direct intention is primarily a volitional state: it concerns what a man wants, either for its own sake or as a means to something else. Of course, as mentioned earlier, if an action is to be voluntary at all then it must be an action which was done because the agent in some sense wanted to do it. But it may be voluntary without being (directly) intentional if it is neither wanted for its own sake nor as a means to any further end. The sense of 'want' in which all voluntary actions is the minimal one elucidated earlier: to say that an agent wants to do X, in this minimal sense, is merely to say that he does X consciously while knowing that it is in his power to refrain from doing X if only he will give up one of his purposes or chosen means. The wanting in question is mere willingness or consent: it is quite different from any feeling of desire, and may be accompanied with varying degrees of enthusiasm diminishing to reluctance and nausea.

Even lawyers who favour the notion of oblique intent for legal purposes agree that for certain crimes direct intent is necessary. Removing a blackout from a window in wartime may assist enemy bombers to find their target: it was remarked in *Steane* that such an action would not be an act done with intent to assist the enemy if it was done merely to ventilate the room. It is sometimes said that oblique intention suffices for crimes of basic intent, while direct intention is necessary for crimes of specific intent. But this distinction is not easy to apply. In the case of many common and serious offences – such as murder and rape – it is not easy to decide whether the crime is one of specific or of basic intent, and whether oblique intention suffices.

Consider first the crime of murder. Murder in common law is killing with malice aforethought: but neither the word 'malice' nor the word 'aforethought' is to be construed in any ordinary sense. Many other kinds of killing count as murder in addition to premeditated malicious killing. Most American jurisdictions allow that the unpremeditated intention to kill or to do grevious bodily harm constitutes malice aforethought in murder, and that a killing can amount to murder even if quite unintentional, if it is caused in the course of the commission of a felony, or as a result of conduct 'evincing a depraved heart, devoid of social duty, and fatally bent on mischief'. An accidental shooting in the course of a robbery would be a felony murder: an instance of depraved heart murder was the case of *Banks* (Texas, 1919) who killed a man while shooting for his own entertainment at the caboose of a passing train. The American model penal code proposed to abolish the category of felony murder, and to define murder as 'causing death purposely or knowingly or recklessly under circumstances manifesting extreme indifference to the value of human life'.[4]

Felony murder was abolished in England by the Homicide Act of 1957, which stated that one who kills another in the course or furtherance of some other offence is not guilty of murder unless the killing is 'done with the same malice aforethought (express or implied) as is required for a killing to amount to murder when not done in the course or furtherance of another offence'. In the case of *Vickers*[5] in the same year, it was ruled that the intention to cause grievous bodily harm, no less than the intention to kill, amounted to malice aforethought.

The intention to kill or do serious injury required for murder has commonly been taken in English law to be oblique, not direct intention; authorities have differed over the degree of certainty required in the foresight constituting the oblique intention. An authority frequently quoted to this effect is the case of *Desmond*[6] (1868). The accused in this case were Fenian conspirators who dynamited a prison wall to liberate their imprisoned colleagues. The plot failed, but the explosion killed persons living nearby. It was no part of the conspirators' plan, either as a means or an end, that anyone should be killed or injured; none the less they were found guilty. The Chief Justice told the jury that it was murder 'if a man did an act ... not with the purpose of taking life, but with the knowledge or belief that life was likely to be sacrificed by it'.

The scope of the English law of murder was widened in 1961 in the case of *Smith*.[7] The accused drove a car in a zig-zag course in order to shake off a policeman clinging to the car: when the policeman suffered fatal injuries the accused was tried and convicted for murder. The House of Lords, restoring the conviction which had been overruled by the Court of Criminal Appeal, handed down a judgment which, in spite of certain obscurities, was widely taken to mean that not even oblique intention was necessary for malice aforethought: if a reasonable man would have foreseen grievous bodily harm as the consequence of the accused's course of action, the accused could be guilty of murder without even obliquely intending either death or grievous bodily harm.

To meet the widespread discontent with the state of the law after *Smith*, the Law Commission in 1967 proposed two reforms.[8] It suggested that no court or jury should be bound to infer that a man intended or foresaw the natural and probable consequences of his actions. It also recommended that killing shall not amount to murder unless done with intent to kill; a man has such an intent 'if he means his actions to kill, or if he is willing for his actions, though meant for another purpose, to kill in accomplishing that purpose'. Had these recommendations been accepted, death which was obliquely intentional would still count as murder: for if one fails to desist from a course of action one knows is likely to cause death, then one is willing for one's actions to kill in accomplishing one's purposes: this is the minimum form of willingness we earlier called 'consent'.

In 1967 the Criminal Justice Act embodied the first, but not the second, of the Law Commission's two proposals. This left the law of homicide in a confused state, since the recommendation about the presumption of intention concerned a reform of the law of evidence, not a definition of murder. In theory the Criminal Justice Act should not have effected the *Smith* ruling: but in practice judges refused to apply it.[9]. The House of Lords was given an opportunity to clarify this confused situation in 1974 in the case of *Hyam*.[10].

The accused in *Hyam*, jealous of a rival who had supplanted her in the affections of her paramour, went to her house in the early hours of the morning, poured petrol through the letterbox, stuffed newspaper through and lit it. She went off leaving the house burning, with the result that two children sleeping in the house were killed. Her defence to the charge of murder was that she had only wanted to frighten her rival into leaving the neighbourhood. She was found guilty, and the conviction was eventually upheld by the House of Lords. The House of Lords is widely held to have ruled that a person who, without intending to endanger life, did an act knowing that it was probable that serious bodily harm would result, was guilty of murder if death resulted. But the exact force of the ruling is not easy to determine. The appeal was dismissed by a majority of three to two, and the three majority judges gave three different accounts of the nature of malice aforethought.

Of the three majority judges Lord Hailsham thought that the intention necessary for murder must be direct intention: but it could be a direct intention to expose a victim to a serious risk of death or grievous bodily harm without necessarily being an intention ˉactually to cause death or grievous bodily harm. Lord Dilhorne and Lord Cross of Chelsea thought that foresight of a likelihood of death sufficed: the former on the grounds that foresight of highly probable consequences amounted to intent, the latter on the grounds that such foresight was an alternative form of malice aforethought. The two minority judges contended that *Vickers* was wrongly decided, and that no act should amount to murder unless committed with at least the awareness that death was likely to result.

Several things are curious about the verdict in *Hyam*. The Court of Criminal Appeal, in giving leave to appeal to the House of Lords, certified that the case involved the following point of law of general public importance:

> Is malice aforethought in the crime of murder established by proof beyond reasonable doubt that when doing the act which led to the death of another the accused knew that it was highly probable that the act would result in death or serious bodily harm?

Though the House of Lords rejected the appeal by three votes to two, the majority of the House thought that the answer to the question certified, in the terms in which it stood, was negative. Lord Hailsham answered it in the negative on the grounds that direct intention was necessary, and that knowledge of high probability was distinct from direct intention. The minority judges, Lords Diplock and Kilbrandon, answered it in the negative on the grounds that foresight of mere serious bodily harm was insufficient for malice aforethought. Those who say that *Hyam* decided that foresight of the probability of grievous bodily harm sufficed for malice aforethought appeal to the fact that four out of five of the judges thought that oblique intention was no less sufficient than direct intention:[11] but even if they are right about this, it cannot be said that the oblique intention of grievous bodily harm is declared by Hyam to be as sufficient for murder as the oblique intention to cause death. For two of the judges thought that it was, and two thought that it was

not: and the fifth judge, Lord Cross of Chelsea, refused to
decide. Having observed that Lord Diplock had argued that
Vickers was wrongly decided, and Lord Dilhorne that it was
correct, he went on to say:

> I am not prepared to decide between them without having
> heard the fullest possible argument on the point from
> counsel on both sides. … For my part, therefore, I shall
> content myself with saying that *on the footing that R v
> Vickers was rightly decided* the answer to the question put
> to us should be 'yes' and that this appeal should be
> dismissed.

Elsewhere, I have argued that after *Hyam* it is not clear
that anything less than the direct intention to kill or to put
life in danger suffices for malice aforethought in murder.[12].
Because of the even division on the topic of *Vickers*, it will
be open for the House of Lords in future, and perhaps even
for lower courts, to rule against the decision that mere intent
to cause grievous bodily harm constitutes malice
aforethought. Because Lord Hailsham's ground for
dismissing the appeal and his answer to the certified question
demanded that there should be direct and not oblique
intention, it will be open for an accused, who caused death
by an act which he foresaw but did not directly intend to be
likely to cause death, to plead that he lacked the necessary
mens rea for murder.

Be that as it may, it seems to me that there is much to be
said for defining murder as causing death by an act done
with the direct intent either to kill or to create a serious risk
to life: the intent to kill being taken to include the (direct)
intent to bring about a state of affairs from which one knows
death will certainly follow.

The difficulty in defining appropriately the *mens rea* for
murder arises from two sides. On the one hand, if it is
defined simply in terms of foresight, then many who are
clearly innocent will be brought within the ambit of the
definition: for instance, a surgeon who undertakes, in order

to save an otherwise doomed life, an operation which has more than a fifty-fifty chance of itself causing death; or a person who drove a car as erratically as Smith, despite the presence of a clinging policeman, in order to remove a time bomb from a populated area. On the other hand, if only the direct intention to cause death is to constitute malice aforethought, a callous criminal who places a bomb on an aeroplane to recover the insurance on its cargo, while entirely indifferent to the fate of the human beings aboard, will have to be acquitted of murder. The definition proposed above, suggested by various remarks in Lord Hailsham's judgment in *Hyam*, avoids both these pitfalls.

I turn now from murder to rape. Rape, it is commonly held, is a crime of basic intent: the *actus reus* of rape is sexual intercourse with a woman (not one's wife) without her consent; the *mens rea* is the intent to do the *actus reus*. The definition of the crime, it will be noticed, is doubly mentalistic: it involves reference to the state of mind of the accused (intent) and of his victim (consent). The 1975 case of *Morgan*[13] brought to light the difficulties which lurk in the apparently simple definition of the crime.

The facts of the case were bizarre, and, one hopes, unusual. A husband, apparently in order to be avenged on his wife for a real or imagined infidelity, invited a number of companions home to have intercourse with her; he urged them to pay no attention to any protest or struggles on her part, as these were simulations designed to increase her sexual satisfaction. The companions, so invited, had intercourse in turn without her consent. They were tried and convicted of rape; in the course of the summing up the judge said:

> The prosecution have to prove that each defendant
> intended to have sexual intercourse with this woman
> without her consent. Not merely that he intended to have
> intercourse with her but that he intended to have
> intercourse without her consent. Therefore if the
> defendant believed or may have believed that Mrs.

Morgan consented to him having sexual intercourse with her, then there would be no such intent in his mind and he would not be guilty of the offence of rape, but such a belief must be honestly held by the defendant in the first place. He must really believe that. And, secondly, his belief must be a reasonable belief; such a belief as a reasonable man would entertain if he applied his mind and thought about the matter.

The accused appealed on the grounds that this was a misdirection. The Court of Appeal held that there was no misdirection, but granted leave to appeal to the House of Lords on the point of general public importance: 'whether in rape the defendant can properly be convicted notwithstanding that he in fact believed that the woman consented if such a belief was not based on reasonable grounds.' Of the five Lords who heard the appeal, two gave an affirmative answer, and three gave a negative answer and held there had been a misdirection. All five, however, dismissed the appeal on the grounds that the misdirection, if misdirection there had been, had led to no miscarriage of justice.

The ruling that an honest belief in consent, however unreasonable, could negate a charge of rape caused considerable public outcry, particularly from feminist groups. The outcry was frequently dismissed by lawyers as based on misunderstanding. In *Smith* the House of Lords had been much criticised for making the beliefs of the reasonable man, as opposed to those of the accused himself, the test of malice aforethought in murder. Was it not now unfair to criticise it for making the beliefs of the accused himself, rather than those of the reasonable man, the test of *mens rea* in rape? How could a man have an intent to have intercourse with a woman without her consent if he honestly believed – however unreasonably – that she was consenting? If women needed protecting against those who unreasonably assumed their consent to intercourse, it was argued, this would be better done by setting up a new offence of non-consensual sexual intercourse rather than by appealing to the law and penalties of rape.

In my view the feminist complaints against the majority ruling in *Morgan* were justified. The decision was a bad one, based on fallacious reasoning. To show this, it is necessary to go into the arguments on both sides of the case in some detail.

The Crown had to show 'an intention to have sexual intercourse with a woman without her consent'. On behalf of the DPP it was argued before the House of Lords that the expression could denote an intention to have sexual intercourse with a woman who is not, in fact, consenting to it. On the other side, Lord Hailsham held that since the *mens rea* for rape was the intent to commit non-consensual sexual intercourse, honest belief clearly negates intent; and the jury must be told that the prisoner is entitled to be acquitted if the intent did not exist. 'Otherwise a jury would in effect be told to find an intent where none existed or where none was proved to have existed. I cannot myself reconcile it with my conscience to sanction as part of the English law what I regard as a logical impossibility'.

Lord Hailsham thought that his statement of the law followed 'as a matter of inexorable logic' from the definition of the law. As it happens, logicians in recent years have given some attention to the problems of drawing inferences from one description of a person's state of mind to another description of the same state. Descriptions of psychological states, such as intention, present the following problem. If we have a true description of someone's beliefs or feelings or intentions which contains a reference to a particular person or event, the description may be changed into a false one if we substitute in it a different manner of referring to the person or event. For instance: I may be glad that the cultural attaché of the USA in London is dining with me; from the fact that, unknown to me, the cultural attaché of the USA in London is the chief agent of the CIA in London it does not follow that I am glad that the chief agent of the CIA in London is dining with me. If, further, the chief agent of the CIA in London is also the chief agent of the KGB in London, it may be that you intend to pass a secret NATO document to the chief agent of the CIA and yet not be true that you intend to pass a secret NATO document to the chief agent of the KGB. This characteristic of the description of mental states and events is called by philosophers 'referential opacity': one cannot, as it were, see through the mode of reference to the person or event referred to. Referential opacity has caught the interest of logicians because, though it is a very simple and elementary phenomenon, it has the consequence that no formal system of mathematical logic yet devised is adequate to deal with inferences concerning mental states and events.

Because of referential opacity, the argument of the DPP must fail. One cannot argue:

> The accused intended to have intercourse with Mrs
> Morgan. Mrs Morgan was a woman who was not
> consenting to intercourse. Therefore, the accused intended
> to have intercourse with a woman who was not
> consenting to intercourse.[14]

Thus far the logic of the majority Lords was superior to that of the Crown. But does logic go on to tell us that the *mens rea* for rape is impossible in the presence of honest belief in consent?

It was recognised explicitly by the House of Lords that the state of mind of someone who does not care whether the woman consents is a sufficient *mens rea* for rape. Lord Simon of Glaisdale (one of the minority) said: 'The *mens rea* is knowledge that the woman is not consenting or recklessness as to whether she is consenting or not.' Lord Hailsham (one of the majority) said: 'the prohibited act is and always has been intercourse without consent of the victim and the mental element is and always has been the intention to commit that act, or the equivalent intention of having intercourse willy-nilly not caring whether the victim consents or no'.

Lord Hailsham in his speech several times distinguished intent in rape from mere knowledge, and referred explicitly to his judgment in *Hyam* in which he equated intent with direct intention. The direct intention to have non-consensual intercourse – where part of what is purposed is that the intercourse should be without consent – must surely be comparatively rare. No doubt it is not impossible: for a particularly sadistic ravisher the unwillingness of the woman may be part of the attractiveness of the prospect of intercourse. But in the case of most of those convicted of rape the state of mind is either knowledge that the woman does not consent (thus merely *oblique* intention to have non-consensual intercourse) or a direct intent to have intercourse whether or not the woman consents.

Now it is true, as Lord Hailsham said, that an honest belief that a woman is consenting will negative an intent (whether direct or oblique) to have intercourse without consent. That is because the belief in consent entails the belief that the intent (whether the sadistic direct intent, or the commoner oblique intent) is incapable of fulfilment while things are as they are believed to be. But an honest belief that a woman consents does not necessarily negate the intent to have intercourse willy-nilly, i.e. the intent to have intercourse *whether or not she consents*. A man may have intercourse with a woman with that intent: if he is lucky, and in fact she does consent, then he is not guilty of rape because he has not committed the *actus reus*. But if that was his frame of mind, then he was prepared to go ahead even if it should have turned out that she did not consent.

The intent to have intercourse whether or not a woman consents appears to be an amalgam of two conditional intents: 'if she consents, I will have intercourse with her' and 'if she does not consent, I will have intercourse with her'. Since by the law of excluded middle either she consents or she does not consent, what makes the difference between the intent to have intercourse willy-nilly, and the simple intent to have intercourse? The difference is a subtle one: to impute one or other intent to a person depends upon a judgment about what he would have done if he had come to believe that she did not consent. Such a judgment may not be easy to make: but it is not always impossible to make it, and one way of arriving at it is to ask what efforts were made to find out whether she consented or not. If the man made no effort, or very little effort, to find out, then it looks as if he did not care whether she consented: and not caring whether she consented is the alternative form of *mens rea* in rape. Now if the belief in consent is an unreasonable one, it must be that, in the words of the trial judge, it was not 'such a belief as a reasonable man would entertain if he applied his mind and thought about the matter'. So whether the belief was reasonable is not simply a piece of evidence about the likelihood that the belief was actually held: even if the belief was honestly held, its unreasonableness may be evidence of that indifference to the woman's consent which is sufficient for *mens rea*. Thus, contrary to the argument of the majority judges, the issue of the reasonableness of the accused's belief can be raised without there being any question of 'finding an intent where none existed'. Since the issue *can* be raised without unfairness to the man, surely it *should* be raised in fairness to the woman. As Lord Simon put it in arguing for an affirmative answer to the question certified: 'A respectable woman who has been ravished would hardly feel that she was vindicated by being told that her assailant must go unpunished because he believed, quite unreasonably, that she was consenting to sexual intercourse with him.'

As a result of public concern about the decision in *Morgan*, the Home Secretary set up the Heilbron committee to inquire whether any change was necessary in the law of rape. The Committee proposed a number of reforms relating to evidence in rape cases, but it did not consider that the majority ruling in Morgan was in principle incorrect. On the contrary, it proposed that the principle of the ruling should be given statutory expression.[15] As a result, the Sexual Offences (Amendment) Act 1976 lays down that '... a man commits rape if (a) he has unlawful sexual intercourse with a woman who at the time of the intercourse does not consent to it; and (b) at the time he knows that she does not consent to the intercourse or he is reckless as to whether she consents to it'.

The effect of the Act does not, in fact, seem to be quite the same as the result of the ruling in *Morgan*. For it seems that an honest belief in consent is in no way incompatible with recklessness about consent; and if that is so an honest but unreasonable belief in consent will not always negate *mens rea* in rape. A working party of the Law Commission offers the following definition of recklessness:[16]

> A person is reckless if (a) knowing that there is a risk that
> an event may result from his conduct, or that a
> circumstance may exist, he takes that risk, and (b) it is
> unreasonable for him to take it , having regard to the
> degree and nature of the risk that he knows to be present.

It is surely perfectly possible that a man might believe that a woman consented while knowing, from the circumstances of the case, that there was a risk that she did not. As he could hardly argue that it was reasonable for him to take the risk, his honest belief would not rebut a charge under the 1976 Act. If it is accepted, for instance, that the defendants in *Morgan* really believed the story they were told by the husband (and the jury seem to have thought they were telling a pack of lies) they must still have known that there was a risk that the victim's complaints and resistance were genuine and not feigned. We may hope, therefore, that the 1976 Act, though it was intended to codify the disastrous decision of the House of Lords, will be found to have had the opposite effect.

Consideration of the law of murder and the law of rape, therefore, illustrates how complicated a matter it may be to specify exactly the *mens rea* for a particular crime. Even in the case of one and the same crime learned judges may differ as to whether the required *mens rea* is ulterior intent or basic intent, direct intent or oblique intent. But in all the cases we have considered, there has been no question but that the *actus reus* must be voluntary: for obliquely intentional consequences, and consequences about which the accused is reckless (i.e. unreasonably accepted obliquely intentional consequences) are all undoubtedly voluntary consequences.

In some cases, acts are punished by the courts which were not themselves voluntary. In most such cases, the non-voluntary acts which are punished are themselves the results of voluntary acts or omissions. The two most common kinds of punishable non-voluntary acts are those which are the result of self-induced capacity, or of voluntary inattention amounting to negligence. In these cases *mens rea* is not totally absent from the accused's history leading up to his criminal action: but it is not a state of mind at the time of the action itself.

Drink and drugs are the commonest causes of self-induced incapacity. In the case of *D.P.P.* v *Majewski*,[17] the facts were as follows. The appellant was involved in a public house brawl in which he was said to have gone berserk. According to his evidence, on the previous day he had consumed two hundred Dexadrine tablets ('speeds') and on the day in question he took about eight sodium nembutal tablets ('barbs'). He then went to the public house. He could remember nothing of what took place there. As a result of the brawl he was accused on three counts of assault occasioning actual bodily harm and three counts of assault on a police constable in the execution of his duty. His defence was that when the assaults were committed he was acting under the influence of drugs and alcohol to such an extent that he did not know what he was doing. The judge at the trial told the jury that this was immaterial: assault was not an offence requiring a specific intent, and therefore self-induced influence of drink and drugs was no defence. The accused was convicted and the conviction upheld at appeal: but leave was granted to appeal to the House of Lords on the point 'whether a defendant may properly be convicted of assault notwithstanding that, by reason of his self-induced intoxication, he did not intend to do the act alleged to constitute the assault'.

The appeal was unanimously dismissed by seven Lords of Appeal. It was accepted, following the judgment of Lord Birkenhead in the case of *Beard*[18] in 1920, that in a case of a crime of specific intent (such as a charge of murder based on intent to kill or do grievous bodily harm) an accused who was so drunk as to be incapable of forming the specific intent could not be convicted. But it was held that since assault was a crime of basic intent, drunkenness provided no defence and the factor of intoxication was irrelevant.

The defence argued that except in the case of offences of strict liability (which did not include assault) no man was guilty of a crime unless he had a guilty mind: a man who when pathologically intoxicated committed what would in ordinary circumstances be a crime lacked a guilty mind and was not criminally culpable for his actions. Though Canadian and American law treated drunken offenders on a par with sober ones, a number of cases in Australia and New Zealand suggested that an unconsciousness of what one was doing, whether or not self-induced, should be treated like epilepsy and diabetic coma which freed from fault.

The Lord Chancellor (Lord Elwyn-Jones) rejecting this defence said that: 'if a man of his own volition took a substance which caused him to cast off the restraints of reason and conscience no wrong was done to him by holding him answerable criminally for any injury he might do while in that condition.' That seems very good sense: but it does not follow that such a person is guilty of the crime of assault. For assault, as the Lord Chancellor expressly said, involves a state of mind in which the accused intended that his acts should cause another person to apprehend immediate and unlawful violence. If, through extreme intoxication, the accused was unable to have such an intent, it is hard to see how he can be guilty of assault. Lord Elwyn-Jones argued that the accused's conduct in reducing himself to that condition supplied the evidence of '*mens rea*: It was a reckless course of conduct, and recklessness was enough to constitute the *mens rea* in assault cases'. This argument seems to equivocate with the word 'reckless'. The recklessness which constitutes *mens rea* in assault is indifference to the foreseen intimidation caused by the actions constituting the assault. The recklessness involved in getting extremely drunk need not involve any foresight of aggressive action, still less of their effects on others. Someone who regularly, when drunk, lays violent hands on those about him may perhaps have the appropriate recklessness for assault as he lays into the bottle for the umpteenth time; but not every drunk becomes violent and therefore not every drunk can be presumed to have the *mens rea* for assault simply on the grounds of his drunkenness.

Of course, the Lord Chancellor was right that it is in no way unjust to hold people responsible for their drunken actions. But there are better ways of doing so than stretching the law of assault and of other crimes of basic intent. The Butler Committee on Mentally Abnormal Offenders recommended that a new offence of 'dangerous intoxication' should be created.[19] It should be an offence, the Committee proposed, for a person while voluntarily intoxicated to do an act or omission that would amount to a dangerous offence if it were done with the requisite state of mind for such an offence. The prosecution would not charge the offence in the first instance, but would charge an offence such as assault under the ordinary law. If evidence of intoxication were given with a view to negating the requisite *mens rea*, the jury could be directed that they might return a verdict of not guilty of assault but guilty of dangerous intoxication. In order to establish that the offence had been committed, the prosecution would not have to establish any mental element with respect to the objectionable behaviour, but it would have to establish that the initial intoxication was not involuntary. Wide discretion should be given to the courts in the disposal of an offender, to take account of the dangerousness of the act committed, and the foreseeability of dangerous action in the light of the accused's record.

Crimes committed as a result of self-induced incapacity are the mirror image of crimes of negligence. In neither case is there any *mens rea* in the sense of knowledge or intent to do the *actus reus* at the time of performing it. But in each case the offence is the result of other voluntary behaviour: in the one case the positive action of inducing intoxication, in the other case the negative omission of failing to pay sufficient attention to enable one to avoid the forbidden course of action. Crimes of negligence include a number of motoring offences: the most serious crime of negligence is negligent homicide, which constitutes involuntary manslaughter. In spite of its name, involuntary manslaughter is always voluntary to the extent of being the result of a voluntary action, or omission. Commonly it is the result of an intentional action performed with some non-homicidal intention.

In going through the various categories of *mens rea* we come finally to crimes of absolute liability in the strict sense: crimes which can be committed without any *mens rea* at the time of the crime (in contrast to crimes of specific or basic intent or causally connected with the crime (in contrast to crimes of self-induced incapacity and negligence). The possession of a forged passport, and the sale of adulterated milk, have already been instanced as examples of such crimes in English law. In such crimes it is no defence to show that one did not know, and could not reasonably have known, that one was doing something which answered to the description of the *actus reus*.

In this chapter I have been analysing the differences between the various types of *mens rea* which are required in the definition of different crimes. On the assumption that distinctions of this kind should be drawn, I have sometimes defended and sometimes criticised the point at which particular laws and particular judgments have drawn the lines between crimes of greater or less gravity. But I have not said anything in defence of the entire apparatus of *mens rea* distinguished from crime to crime. Such a defence will be the task of chapter 4.[17]

The question concerning *mens rea* from which we started these lectures can now be reformulated as follows. Should all crimes be crimes of strict liability, so that *mens rea* should be totally abolished (as many social reformers have argued); or should no crimes be crimes of strict liability (as some civil libertarians have argued)? Or should we preserve the system which we now have, in which for some crimes *mens rea* is required and for some it is not?

To answer this question we must reflect on the purpose of the criminal law and of the penal system as a whole. To this the final chapter will be devoted.

NOTES

1 [1964] A.C. 763.
2 [1947] K.B. 997.
3 See Lord Simon of Glaisdale in *Morgan* (1975 2 All E.R. 347).
4 J.A. La Fave and H.P. Scott, *Criminal Law*, Bobbs-Merrill, Indianapolis, 1971, pp. 528ff.
5 [1957] 2 All E.R. 741.
6 *The Times*, 28 April 1868.
7 [1961] A.C. 290.
8 *Imputed Criminal Intent* (D.P.P. v Smith), 1967, pp. 16–17.
9 See Buxton, 'The Retreat from Smith', *The Criminal Law Review*, 1966, pp. 195ff.
10 [1974] 2 All E.R. 41.
11 See Buxton, 'Malice Aforethought', *The Modern Law Review*, 1974, pp. 676–81.
12 In 'Intention and *Mens Rea* in Murder', *Law, Morality and Society*, ed P. Hacker and J. Raz, Oxford University Press, 1977.
13 [1975] 2 All E.R. 347.
14 The argument illustrates referential opacity in a broader sense than that customary among logicians, since the second premiss is not an identity statement.
15 *Report of the Advisory Group on the Law of Rape*, Cmnd 6352, 1975.
16 Working Party Report no. 31, *The Mental Element in Crime*, Law Commission 1974.
17 [1976] W.L.R., 625.
18 [1970] A.C. 479.
19 *Report of the Committee on Mentally Abnormal Offenders* (Butler committee), Cmd 6244, 1975, ch. 18.

4 Reason, deterrence and punishment

We come finally to the moral justification of the concept of responsibility. Responsibility, in the appropriate sense, is liability to punishment; and so the justification of responsibility is closely connected with the justification of punishment.

Theories of punishment are sometimes divided into retributive theories, deterrent theories and remedial theories.

The remedial theories frequently take the form of denying that there is any such thing as a just punishment: the task of society is to cure its criminals, not to punish. The remedial theory, in so far as it is a justification of punishment at all, sees the justification in terms of the improvement of the criminal. The great weakness of the remedial theories as a justification of actual penal practice is that so few of the current punishments inflicted on criminals can have any serious claim to do any good to them or improve them in any way.

In this chapter I shall take it for granted that there are some punishments which are just: hence I shall not be concerned with remedial theories in the sense indicated. Retributive and deterrent theories have as common ground the assertion that punishment may be justly inflicted; they differ in their explanation of what constitutes the justice of a just punishment.

The retributive theory of punishment is very difficult to state accurately. Indeed, I shall be concerned to argue that it is impossible to state it coherently: but this must be the result, and not the premiss, of our investigation. I shall begin, therefore, by stating the theory as baldly as possible, and then go on to consider the defects of the theory so stated with a view to discovering whether they can be refined away.

To avert misunderstanding, I should remark that there can be no objection to saying that a person who is justly punished for a crime has met with just retribution. The question at issue is whether the notion of 'just punishment' is to be explained by means of the notion of 'retribution' or vice versa. According to the retributive theory of punishment which I wish to criticise, 'retribution' is not a synonym for 'punishment' (or a genus of which reward and punishment are species), but rather a quite independent concept which serves as an explanation of the justice of a just punishment. The essence of the retributive theory is an assimilation of the word 'just' as it occurs in 'just punishment' to the use of it in such phrases as 'just price' and 'just wage'. On this theory, the relation of crime to punishment is the same as that between merchandise and money, services and salary, or work and wages. The theory of retributive justice is an attempt to give an account of the justice of a just punishment in terms of commutative justice.

Justice demands – so the theory runs – that he who has done harm shall suffer harm. Independently of any deterrent or remedial effect which the criminal's suffering may have on himself or others, justice is better served if the criminal is made to suffer than if he is allowed to go scot free. Each man must be done by as he has done. What a man sows, that let him reap. Ideally, he should suffer exactly as much harm as he has done. Fallible human justice rarely achieves this ideal: being unable, in many cases, to measure the exact harm done, human authority has to be content with broad approximation. The infallible judgments of God, on the other hand, proportion the punishment exactly to the crime of the sinner.

Stated thus crudely, of course, the theory does not sound

in the least convincing. It is given plausibility by the use of metaphors, in particular the metaphor of balance and the metaphor of payment. By his crime, we are told, the criminal has upset the balance of justice; by his punishment the balance is restored. By his sin, the sinner incurs a debt; by his subsequent sufferings, this debt is paid off.

These two metaphors exercise a powerful hold on our imagination. That hold can be broken only by making the metaphors as explicit as possible, and treating them with complete seriousness.

Let us take first the metaphor of the balance. Painters portray even-handed justice, blindfold, carrying a pair of scales. This is not the picture which is in question here. Justice, in the metaphor, is neither the weigher nor the scales; justice is the even balance of the scales. When the scales are evenly balanced, justice has been done; when one or other pan is overweight, the scale tilts, and the equilibrium which constitutes justice is disturbed. Into one pan of the scales are put a man's actions; into the other pan is put what happens to him. By his wrongful act, the criminal tilts the scales; into the other pan goes his punishment, and the scales are brought back into the horizontal. As long as the crime goes unpunished, the scale remains tilted and justice unsatisfied. To restore the balance, the punishment must be equal and apposite to the crime.

Clearly, such a picture could not serve as an explanation of the justice of a just punishment. If we have already explained what a just punishment is, we may be able to illustrate our explanation by using some such pictorial representation. But a metaphor cannot take the place of an explanation.

Even as an illustration, the metaphor of the balance is open to serious objection. We may note, first, that such a picture leaves no room at all for mercy: as long as the criminal's misdeeds have not been balanced by his sufferings, the scales remain out of equilibrium. Mercy would not be a virtue: it would be an accessory of injustice.

Perhaps we can add elements to the picture to overcome

this defect; but there is a second, more radical, difficulty which no tinkering can remedy. It is essential to the metaphor that what goes into one pan must be equal and opposite to what goes into the other pan. That is to say, the only difference between what the criminal does and what he suffers must be precisely that in the one case it is his action, and in the other his suffering. But how are we to describe what he does and what he suffers? If we give a purely physical description, then what he does will not be a crime; if we give a moral description, then what he suffers will not be a punishment. In stating the theory earlier, I chose the first horn of this dilemma: he who does harm must suffer harm. But clearly, this will not do, since only the *wrongful* infliction of harm may justly be punished. On the other hand, it is equally clear that we cannot state the principle of retribution thus: he who does harm wrongfully must suffer harm wrongfully. For the retributive theory was meant to explain, and the balance metaphor to illustrate, how he who has done harm wrongfully may suffer harm *rightfully*. Once punishment and crime have to be described in different terms, then the notion of retribution loses its plausibility, and the balance picture its appropriateness.

The second illustrative metaphor – that of payment – is used in two ways. Sometimes, the criminal is regarded as contracting by his crime a debt which is paid off when he is punished. Alternatively, the crime may be looked upon as a piece of labour, for which the grim reward of punishment is due. The wages of sin is death.

This metaphor has its place: but it is not that of explaining what constitutes a just punishment. It has the disadvantage of suggesting that justice is equally well deserved if crime is punished as if no crime is committed at all. But clearly, a society in which there are no criminals is a juster society than a society in which every citizen is a criminal and every citizen is punished. In the first of the two forms given above, the payment metaphor has the advantage over the balance metaphor of leaving a place for mercy. A debt may be remitted just as a crime may be forgiven. None the less there

are other difficulties peculiar to this metaphor. It is by no
means clear to whom the debt is due. One would expect the
offender's debt to be to the person whom he has injured. But
if A has assaulted B he cannot avoid sentence on the grounds
that B has forgiven him for his attack. Should we say then
that the debt is owed to society? But in what way does
society profit from the suffering of one of its members,
unless that suffering is either deterrent or remedial?

This brings us to the crucial argument against any purely
retributive theory of punishment. The essential element in
punishment, according to such a theory, is the harming of
the criminal, whether in his life, liberty, or property. This
harm is sought directly as an end in itself, and not as a means
to deter or correct. But to seek the harm of another as an end
in itself is the paradigm case of an unjust action. Retribution
of this kind would not restore any balance of justice or
square any accounts. It would increase, instead of
diminishing, the amount of injustice in the world. Popular
wisdom, which has many adages which seem to favour the
retributive theory, has one which is conclusive against it:
two wrongs don't make a right. We must not render evil
for evil.

An upholder of the retributive theory would protest that
the criminal's suffering is sought not as an end in itself, but
as a means to the restoration of justice. But this is to trifle.
For on the retributive theory all that 'the restoration of
justice' *means* is that the criminal is to suffer in proportion to
his crime. The restoration of justice is not some further,
separately identifiable, end to which the offender's sufferings
are a means – it *is* those sufferings, in these circumstances;
just as when money is handed over to pay a debt, the
payment of the debt is not some further, separately
identifiable, end to which the handing over of the money is a
means, but *is* that handing over, in the circumstances in
which it takes place.

Oddly enough, the root of the error contained in the
retributive theory of punishment is the same as the root of
the error contained in the purely remedial theory. Both

theories attempt to give an account of crime and punishment as two episodes in a criminal's life, considered in isolation both from the authority imposing the punishment and the society in which the criminal lives. The retributive theory, starting from the premiss that it is just to punish, reaches the conclusion that it is just to render evil for evil. The remedial theory, starting from the premiss that it is unjust to render evil for evil, reaches the conclusion that it is unjust to punish.

Both premisses are true; they lead to false conclusions only if punishment is considered in isolation from authority. On this there is general agreement: but it is not always noticed that the principle is a matter of logic, and not of morals. 'Punishment may be imposed only by authority' is not the same sort of sentence as 'sexual intercourse is unlawful with girls under thirteen'. Connection with authority is not something extraneous to punishment; it is part of its essence. There is not some independently identifiable activity known as punishing, which is legitimate only when exercised by authority, as there is an independently identifiable activity of sexual intercourse which is illicit if it takes place with a girl under thirteen. No activity whatever can be rightly called 'punishing' unless it is performed by authority.

Clearly, we would not be willing to describe as 'punishment' just *any* misfortune which fell upon a wrongdoer subsequent to his misdeeds. A murderer who falls to his death down a manhole before arrest has escaped punishment, not suffered it. A slanderer who suffers an attack of lumbago for a week after uttering his slander cannot escape sentence on the plea that he has already been punished for his crime. A fraudulent promoter who loses the fruits of his crimes at chemin-de-fer has not thereby done any service to justice. Of course, someone may say that such misfortunes are providential punishments for the sins which preceded them. But to see the hand of God in the fortuitous or self-inflicted miseries of criminals is *eo ipso* to see these sufferings as proceeding from authority.

Sufferings consequent upon misdoing, even if imposed

precisely on account of the misdeeds, is still not punishment unless those who inflict it have authority over the offender. A child who revenges himself on cruel parents by strewing thistles in their bed is not thereby punishing his parents, however much their cruelty may have merited punishment. A man who injures a fellow-man out of spite may well say, 'I did it to punish him'; but in saying this he is arrogating to himself an authority over his victim. He is, literally, adding insult to injury.

If it is a mistake to separate punishment from the authority which imposes it, it is equally a mistake to regard its infliction as being, in general, for the sake of the criminal. I say 'for the sake of', for the mistake occurs equally whether one thinks of the purpose of punishment as being to benefit the criminal or whether one regards it as directed to harming him. The purpose of parental punishment is indeed to benefit the child. It aims to benefit him by curing him of whatever vice he is being punished for; and it cures him, if it cures him, by deterring him from repeating his offence.

But the purpose of society's punishment of criminals is not primarily, or necessarily at all, to benefit the criminal. Nor is it to benefit the law-abiding citizens, by protecting them from 'the criminal classes'. It is for the benefit of every citizen as such, but its benefit to him is indirect. The threat of punishment benefits the citizen 'by deterring himself and others from the commission of crime, and thus helping to enforce the laws which are drawn up for the benefit of the community as a whole. The exaction of punishment benefits the citizen by ensuring that the threat of punishment is not an empty threat.

The problem 'What constitutes the justice of a just punishment?' is not quite the same as the problem 'How should society treat those who have broken its laws?' The problem of punishment is sometimes stated as if it were a problem about the attitude which society should adopt to a specific minority, namely the class of criminals. But society does not contain a class of criminals in the same way as it may contain a class of Jews or Catholics. The class of criminals is defined, as the class of Jews and the class of Catholics are not, partly by the attitude which society takes up towards the members of the class. There are many attitudes which a society may take up towards ethnic or religious minorities; but the only attitude which it can adopt towards the class of criminals is to aim to eliminate it. A criminal is, by definition, a member of a class which society wishes to have no members.

To be sure, society is unlikely to succeed in its aim: crime is always with us. But we cannot disguise our failure in this aim by pretending that it is success in some other aim. The primary purpose of punishment is to prevent citizens from becoming criminals; hence punishment will never be understood if it is regarded purely as a transaction between society and those who have already become criminals. When a man is punished, the purpose of punishment has, in his case, already been thwarted. The most effective punishment is one which never has to be inflicted. 'Trespassers will be prosecuted' is an announcement which is best verified by there being no trespassers and no prosecutions.

In saying that the problem of how to treat offenders is not the same as the problem of the justification of punishment, I do not, of course, wish to suggest that it is a false or trivial problem. It is one of the most difficult questions facing society: but it is a question which cannot be answered merely by a theory of punishment. What is done by society to offenders must be deterrent, if it is to be punishment at all; but society has not fulfilled all justice merely by providing deterrents from crime.

Those who oppose the deterrent theory of punishment often pose one very simple and fundamental objection: deterrent penalties, they say, do not in fact deter. They point to the high rate of recidivisim in all crimes, and the apparent ineffectiveness of even the supreme penalty of death in affecting the murder rates within a given jurisdiction.

The objections are in large measure based on misunderstanding. In the first place, the deterrent effect of punishment is not to be measured by its effects on those who have already been punished and return to commit further crime. The major deterrent effect claimed for punishment is on the population as a whole, deterring all of us when tempted to crime from committing it in the first place. Those who commit even a first crime have thereby shown themselves to be less deterrable than the rest of the population: they are therefore a biassed sample to choose for study. The only empirical way to study the deterrent effect of punishment would be to compare the effects of two laws in parallel jurisdictions on the same type of subject matter, one of which had a sanction attached and the other did not. Naturally, it is difficult to find legislatures foolish enough to provide the circumstances in which such statistics can be collected.

Anyone who thinks that the imposition of sanctions has no effect on people's behaviour should consider the case of Prohibition in the USA. The ban on alcohol was one of the least successful pieces of legislation in US history: it attempted to bring the force of penal deterrence to bear in a field where the strength of addiction was great. The measure failed to a great extent in its purpose of making US citizens give up drinking alcohol: but even those who were the keenest customers of the bootleggers, and continued most doggedly in their drinking habits, changed their behaviour over a wide area of their lives in substantial ways in order to avoid the sanctions attached to drinking by the criminal law. What is true of this disastrously inept piece of legislation is true *a fortiori* in other cases.

Sceptics about deterrence have often concentrated their attention on particular crimes such as murder and particular punishments such as the death penalty. Murder appears to be an uncharacteristic crime in being less affected than other offences by variations in penal practice. Naturally, there are no statistics for jurisdictions where murder goes unpunished by law; hence the murder statistics can at most tell us about the effectiveness of different penalties, not about the effectiveness of punishment as such.

Opponents of deterrence theories are right to insist that it is an empirical matter how far particular punishments deter: it is risky to argue *a priori* what is the appropriate tariff of punishment to reduce the rate of crime. An excellent passage of such *a priori* argument is to be found in Lord Macaulay's 'Notes on the Indian Penal Code',[1] where he is arguing in favour of the death penalty for murder and for murder alone.

> We are of opinion that to put robbers, ravishers and mutilators on the same footing with murderers is an arrangement which diminishes the security of life. There is in practice a close connexion between murder and most of the offences which come nearest to murder in enormity. Those offences are almost always committed under such circumstances that the offender has it in his power to add murder to his guilt. The same opportunities, the same superiority of force, which enabled a man to rob, to mangle or to ravish, will enable him to go further and to dispatch his victim. As he has almost always the power to murder, he will often have a strong motive to murder, inasmuch as by murder he may often hope to remove the only witness of the crime which he has already committed. If the punishment of the crime which he has already committed be exactly the same with the punishment of murder, he will have no restraining motive. A law which imprisons for rape and robbery, and hangs for murder, holds out to ravishers and robbers a strong inducement to spare the lives of those whom they have injured. A law which hangs for rape and robbery and only hangs for murder, holds out indeed if it be rigorously carried into effect a strong motive to deter men from rape and robbery; but as soon as a man has ravished or robbed it holds out to him a strong motive to follow up his crime with a murder.

Macaulay, of course, was writing at a time in which many other crimes other than murder carried the death penalty: he was arguing that the death penalty should be restricted to murder alone. His argument seems persuasive: but is it the case in fact that a legal system including capital punishment deters from murder more effectively than a legal system otherwise comparable which lacks the death penalty? The British Royal Commission on Capital Punishment collected in 1949 and 1950 evidence from many jurisdictions: it concluded that there was no clear evidence in any of the countries that abolition of the death penalty had led to an increase in the homicide rate, or that its reintroduction had led to a fall. The death penalty was effectively abolished in England and Wales in 1965. Between 1961 and 1974 the number of offences recorded by the police as murder rose from 214 to 520. Most such offences are usually found by a court to be manslaughter; the number of offences found by courts to be murder rose in the same period from 38 to 148. These increases appear impressive: but during the same period the rates for other offences were increasing even more sharply. In the state of Delaware the death penalty was introduced, after four years of abolition, in 1961, after a series of brutal murders. It has turned out that the rate of murders during the years of abolition was lower than before or since. Altogether, the evidence about the deterrent effect of the death penalty is inadequate and ambiguous.[2] Some types of murder may perhaps be more easily deterrable than others. In the absence of a strong case for the death penalty being a uniquely effective deterrent, most people feel that more humane counsels should prevail.

Once one has set out what is involved in the attribution of *mens rea* (namely, an inquiry into the agent's reasons for his action) and what is the purpose of punishment (the provision of reasons for abstaining, through fear, from anti-social action) the connection between *mens rea* and responsibility becomes self-evident: the two concepts fit together like a key and a lock. The connection between the deterrent purpose of punishment and the necessity of *mens rea* if a crime is to be imputed is made *via* the concept of practical reasoning: the attachment of penal sanction to legislation is precisely an attempt to affect the practical reasoning of citizens.

Mental illness which incapacitates from practical reasoning, therefore, both excludes *mens rea* and exempts from responsibility. This has long been recognised in the traditional defence of insanity: it is for this reason that the M'Naghten rules were framed in the way they were. Such a recognition is quite different from the fashionable attitude that the structure of crime and punishment should be replaced by that of illness and treatment. So far as possible citizens who are capable of reasoning should be appealed to by means of reason, rather than causally acted upon like irrational agents. The forcible incarceration of the dangerously insane is not a violation of this principle. In the normal case of punishment the notion of treatment is an inappropriate one, just as the notion of illness is an inappropriate one in the normal case of crime. The concept of mental illness in our day is constantly being so extended that it loses all meaning, or turns into a condescendingly emotive description of tendencies to behave in ways of which the describer disapproves. This inane extension of the concept should be resisted. As I have written elsewhere:[3]

> In the paradigmatic case of illness the causes, symptoms and remedies of disease are all physical. In the paradigmatic cases of mental illness (e.g. schizophrenia) organic causes are known or suspected, and treatment by physical methods (drugs, electroconvulsive therapy) is at least partially effective. What make such illnesses mental illnesses is that the symptoms concern the cognitive and affective life of the patient: disorders of perception, belief and emotion. In the diagnosis of whether perception is normal, or whether belief is rational, or whether emotion is out of proportion, there is a gentle slope which leads from clinical description to moral evaluation. Still, in such cases, even where diagnosis is as it were infected with morality, the relation to organic causes and physical treatment is strong enough to give clear content to the concept of disease. But some would like to broaden the

concept of mental illness in such a way that crime by itself becomes indefeasible evidence for disease. No scientific justification has ever been provided for such a move. If a psychopath is given psychotherapy then neither the alleged causes of the condition (e.g. a broken home) nor its symptoms (petty theft) nor its cure (client centred group discussions) have anything in common with the causes, symptoms or cure of organic diseases. In such a case the concept of mental illness has become a mere metaphor; and whatever value these procedures may have must be capable of commendation by something other than metaphor.

Few of those who are actually concerned with the administration of the law look with favour on such a boundless extension of the notion of mental illness. None the less, it is a widely held view that the M'Naghten rules err on the other side by offering an excessively narrow definition of the circumstances in which it is proper for 'disease of the mind' to free from criminal responsibility. Certainly a person can suffer from a severe mental illness, such that he would be regarded by almost anyone as being quite mad, and yet not necessarily satisfy the M'Naghten conditions of not knowing the nature and quality of the acts he does, or their moral and legal status. Such mental illness will not necessarily incapacitate from all practical reasoning. Should it exempt from criminal responsibility, and if so when?

A natural answer is that it should exempt from responsibility for those of the accused's actions for which it is itself responsible: in a formula which once found favour in the USA, the accused should not be criminally responsible 'if his unlawful act is the product of mental disease or mental defect'. The Butler Committee on Mentally Abnormal Offenders considered this proposal, but rejected it on the grounds that it was difficult to be certain how much of a person's behaviour is affected by mental disorders that he may suffer. Instead, following the lead of the Code Napoleon, it suggested that severe mental disorder should

free completely from criminal responsibility, and that when
the jury believes that the accused, at the time of his alleged
criminal act, was suffering from severe mental illness or
severe subnormality they should bring in a verdict of 'not
guilty on evidence of mental disorder'. The court would
have wide discretion in disposal after such a special verdict,
having in its power a number of alternatives from committal
to a secure hospital to absolute discharge.

According to the Butler proposals, a special verdict could
be reached in two different ways.[4] In the first place, evidence
of mental disorder may go to show that the accused lacked
the *mens rea* for the particular crime with which he is
charged. The jury should bring in the special verdict if they
find that the defendant did the act or made the omission
charged but (by reason of the evidence of mental disorder)
they do not find that the state of mind required for the
offence has been proved and they further find that on the
balance of probabilities the defendant was mentally
disordered at the time.

In the second place, evidence of mental disorder may
prevent the conviction of someone who, but for that
evidence, has been shown by the prosecution to have
performed the prohibited act with the appropriate *mens rea*.
The special verdict should be returned, despite the
prosecution case, if the jury believe that at the time of the act
or omission charged the defendant was suffering from severe
mental illness or severe subnormality. The Committee gives
a commendably specific list of the conditions to be fulfilled if
something is to count as a 'severe mental illness'.

The Committee are well aware of the radical nature, in a
common law context, of the proposal that mental disorder
should free from responsibility for a crime with which it has,
on the face of it, no connection whatever. 'It is true', they
say, 'that it is theoretically possible for a person to be
suffering from a severe mental disorder which has in a
causal sense nothing to do with the act or omission for
which he is punished; but in practice it is very difficult to
imagine a case in which one could be sure of the absence of

such a connection.' On the basis of the difficulty of being sure that there is no connection, the Committee then go on to establish a presumption that there *is* a connection, and a presumption which, if their proposals mean what they appear to mean, is an irrebuttable one.

This seems a rash step. Let us suppose that an academic suffers from paranoid delusions that his colleagues are constantly plagiarising his work, and that they are denying him unjustly the promotion that is due to his talents (which in his own deluded opinion amount to near-genius). This will bring him within the Butler Committee's definition of a severely mentally disordered person. Let us suppose that while subject to these delusions he makes careful and efficient plans for the secret poisoning of his mother-in-law so that he and his wife can enjoy the large fortune which they stand to inherit by her death. It does not seem at all obvious that his mental disorder should excuse him from criminal responsibility for a premeditated murder which has no connection with it. No doubt his mental disorder entitles him to sympathy from those more fortunate. He would be equally entitled to sympathy if he was blind or had lost the use of his legs: but that would not exempt him from criminal responsibility.

The Butler Committee, to show the excessive narrowness of the M'Naghten Rules, points out that some severe mental disorders do not prevent the sufferer from forming positive intentions and carrying them out efficiently. 'An instance would be a person who killed someone quite deliberately but under the delusion that he had been ordered by God to do so.' The instance seems uncommonly ill-chosen. Such a person would fit without any strain under the M'Naghten exemption of one 'labouring under such a defect of reason, from disease of the mind ... that he did not know he was doing what was wrong.'

The M'Naghten rules recognise that even those with severe mental illnesses conduct a great part of their lives in accordance with practical reasoning in the light of the alternatives open to them and the consequences of those alternatives. To the extent that they can do so, they can be influenced by the penalties which the law holds out for intentional wrongdoing. To the extent that their delusions vitiate their reasoning by disguising from them the nature of what they are doing, or the moral and legal consequences of their actions, they will fall within the exemptions provided by the M'Naghten rules. Beyond this, there is nothing unjust to them in holding them criminally responsible for their actions: and there may well be an injustice to others in removing from them the deterrents which the law holds out to the sane.

It may well be replied that the existence of the Butler special verdict will in no way weaken any existing deterrent effect of criminal penalties. The indeterminacy of disposal after a special verdict, including the possibility of indefinite confinement in a secure mental hospital, may be as unattractive a prospect as any of the punishments meted out to those criminally responsible. There will therefore be no temptation to the mentally disordered to feel that they have been licensed to commit acts prohibited to the less afflicted, and no temptation to the sane to trump up evidence of mental disorder at their trial in order to exchange a conviction for a special verdict. To the extent that this is true, it seems that the Butler proposals, so far from being compassionate, may actually be unjust to the mentally disordered. There must be many who suffer from disorders severe enough to bring them within the Butler exemptions from responsibility, but not severe enough to render it necessary, provided they abstain from unlawful action, to confine them against their will. Why should their illness be a reason for depriving them of that security against indefinite compulsory confinement that is provided to all other citizens who abstain from crimes carrying a life sentence?

The general principle, then, that responsibility should extend as far as *mens rea* extends, can be applied without injustice to the mentally disordered no less than to the sane. In so far as the afflictions of the mentally disordered make them incapable of being susceptible to the deterrents provided by the law, they make them also incapable of the states of mind constituting the *mens rea* of the various crimes.

In the same way as the justification of the general requirement of *mens rea* flows from the nature of punishment and the nature of practical reasoning, so the justification of distinguishing between different degrees of *mens rea* arises from the different degrees of proximity to the actuality or possibility of practical reasoning in particular criminal behaviour. The same act, when performed negligently, may be punished less severely than when performed knowingly, and the same act when performed recklessly may be punished less severely than when performed intentionally. We must ask why this is so, and whether it should be so.

Negligent actions, it was said earlier, are actions which are performed unknowingly as a result of voluntary acts or omissions. Commonly a negligent action is the result of the voluntary omission to acquire the relevant item of knowledge: a negligent killing, for instance, is the result of the failure to ascertain the lethal nature of one's action. A negligent action can be regarded as itself voluntary in the sense of being the result of not caring sufficiently about what one is doing to ascertain its nature: this is why negligence can be regarded as a form of *mens rea* and why it is just to punish negligent actions.

The punishment of negligent actions can be regarded as a special case of the punishment of omissions: in this case, the omission to acquire the requisite knowledge about what one is doing. The general issue of the punishment of omissions was addressed by Macaulay in his 'Notes on the Indian Penal Code'.[5] It was evident, Macaulay said, that some omissions should be punishable no less than acts, and others, though equally productive of evil effects, should not be. On what principle should one decide which should be punishable?

It is difficult to say whether a penal code which should put no omissions on the same footing with acts, or a penal code which should put all omissions on the same footing with acts, would produce consequences more absurd and revolting. There is no country in which either of these principles is adopted. Indeed, it is hard to conceive how, if either were adopted, society could be held together.

What we propose is this, that where acts are made punishable on the ground that they have caused, or have been intended to cause, or have been known to be likely to cause, a certain evil effect, omissions which have caused, which have been intended to cause, or which have been known to be likely to cause the same effect, shall be punishable in the same manner, provided that such omissions were, on other grounds, illegal. An omission is illegal ... if it be an offence, if it be a breach of some direction of law, or if it be such a wrong as would be a good ground for a civil action.

We cannot defend this rule better than by giving a few illustrations of the way in which it will operate. A. omits to give Z. food, and by that omission voluntarily causes Z.'s death. Is this murder? Under our rule it is murder if A. was Z.'s gaoler, directed by the law to furnish Z. with food. It is murder if Z. was the infant child of A., and had therefore a legal right to sustenance, which right a Civil Court would enforce against A. It is murder if Z. was a bedridden invalid, and A. a nurse hired to feed Z. It is murder if A. was detaining Z. in unlawful confinement, and had thus contracted a legal obligation to furnish Z., during the continuance of the confinement, with necessaries. It is not murder if Z. is a beggar, who has no other claim on A. than that of humanity. ...

We are sensible that in some of the cases which we have put, our rule may appear too lenient; but we do not think that it can be made more severe without disturbing the whole order of society. It is true that the man who, having abundance of wealth, suffers a fellow-creature to die of hunger at his feet is a bad man, a worse man, probably, than many of those for whom we have provided very severe punishment. But we are unable to see where, if we make such a man legally punishable, we can draw the line. ...

It is, indeed, most highly desirable that men should not merely abstain from doing harm to their neighbours, but should render active services to their neighbours. In general, however, the penal law must content itself with keeping men from doing positive harm, and must leave to public opinion, and to the teachers of morality and religion, the office of furnishing men with motives for doing positive good. It is evident that to attempt to punish men by law for not rendering to others all the service which it is their duty to render to others would be preposterous. We must grant impunity to the vast majority of those omissions which a benevolent morality would pronounce reprehensible, and must content ourselves with punishing such omissions only when they are distinguished from the rest by some circumstance which marks them out as peculiarly fit objects of penal legislation. Now, no circumstance appears to us so well fitted to be the mark as the circumstance which we have selected. It will generally be found in the most atrocious cases of omission; it will scarcely ever be found in a venial case of omission; and it is more clear and certain than any other mark that has occurred to us. That there are objections to the line which we propose to draw, we have admitted. But there are objections to every line which can be drawn, and some line must be drawn.

This last point is of wide application. In general more serious crimes should have more serious punishments; but not every crime in a more serious category (e.g. murder) will be morally worse than one in a less serious category (e.g. manslaughter): terminating the life of a suffering and hopeless patient may well be morally better than recklessly aiming a gun at the caboose of passing trains. This possibility is something which no care and skill in legislation can exclude: it can be provided for only by flexibility in conditions for disposal and sentencing.

Punishment of negligent action is punishment of the failure to take care, which itself sets the standard which the care is to reach and lays down the positive obligation of achieving it. The standard is set in the simplest way by specifying the mischief that the care is to avoid (e.g. the likelihood of accident, in careless driving, and the death of a human being, in manslaughter). The moral justification for the punishment of negligent action has recently been well expressed by A. Woozley:[6]

> There is nothing inherently unfair about punishing a man for performing a prohibited act, which he performed neither purposely nor knowingly, if it was his own fault that he did not know; and sometimes it is his own fault. And the prospect of punishment, although it will not directly deter him from an action which has an outcome that he neither intends nor expects, may induce him to be more careful about finding out, or more cautious about acting in situations in which he has not found out. The knowledge that 'I didn't know' will not be accepted as an excuse in situations where he could have known (i.e. where he had opportunity and power) can make a difference to a person who is otherwise disinclined to bother.

The justification for punishing negligence is clear. But what is the justification for punishing recklessness more severely than negligence? 'Recklessness' is sometimes used to denote an attitude of not caring, not troubling to find out the consequences of one's actions when one should: in that case it is a form of negligence. But here the word is being used as the Law Commission suggested that it should, to mean the knowing acceptance of risk. Killing which is reckless in this sense – which is the result of actions undertaken in the knowledge that they are lethally dangerous – will in most jurisdictions be more heavily punished, as murder, than killing which is the result of negligent action, which will count as manslaughter. Why should this be so?

No doubt almost everyone would regard a reckless killer as more wicked than an inadvertent killer; but the law's principal concern is the prevention of harm, and the harm done by either killer is identical. Should not the penalty too be identical? No: for the point at which the threat of punishment is intended to be brought to bear upon practical reasoning is different in the two cases. The threat of punishment for negligence is meant to enforce at all times a standard of care to ensure that one's actions do not endanger life: the threat of punishment for recklessness is meant to operate at the specific points at which one is contemplating a course of action known to be life-endangering. The actions, therefore, on which the threat of punishment for negligence is brought to bear are less dangerous than those on which the threat of punishment for recklessness is brought to bear: for in general actions which, for all one knows, may be dangerous are less dangerous than actions which one positively knows to be a risk to life. Hence the more severe threat of punishment is held out to the citizen contemplating the more dangerous action.

Just as actions known to be likely to cause death are in general more dangerous than those not known not to be so likely, so actions done with the intention of causing death are in general more dangerous than those merely foreseen as likely to cause death. (The latter, for instance, unlike the former, are compatible with the taking of precautions against the causing of death.) This perhaps offers a reason for punishing intentional homicide more severely than reckless homicide, just as reckless homicide is punished more severely than negligent homicide. Few jurisdictions make as sharp a distinction between intentional and reckless homicide as they do between reckless and negligent homicide. Should they do so?

The consideration that acts intended to cause death are more dangerous than acts done with foresight of death would not justify making any distinction between penalties in cases where the result, though unintended, is foreseen as certain: for in such cases the danger is obviously the same in each case. There may be important moral differences between acts done to achieve a certain result and acts done with mere foresight of that result: there is, for instance, a clear moral difference between the case of a judge who sends a man to prison knowing that this will cause hardship to his wife and that of a judge who sends a man to prison *in order that* he may cause hardship to the wife, against whom he has some grudge. But where an evil effect is foreseen as certain it is quite reasonable that it should in law be treated as if it had been intended. On the other hand, in most jurisdictions the law punishes acts intended to bring about an evil effect more severely than acts done in consciousness of a risk of the evil effect in cases where the probability is in each case rather slight. A shot which is most unlikely to kill or injure anyone will, if by chance it does cause death, be treated as murder if it was intended to kill, as manslaughter if it was not; if it is spent harmlessly no offence will be committed if there was no intent to kill, with intent it will amount to the crime of attempt.

The difficult question is this: should the law punish intentional homicide more severely than reckless killing when the antecedent probability is high but falls short of certainty?[7] A law which does not make any distinction does already, of course, provide incentives for taking precautions against death in cases where death is not intended. It is only in rather special cases in which making a distinction between the severity of the punishments for the two types of offence will affect the practical reasoning of potential killers.

Let us suppose that a potential criminal wishes to achieve a certain goal – not necessarily in itself prohibited – and he has two means open to him to achieve the goal. Let us suppose that one involves killing someone but makes the achievement of the goal certain, while the other involves a 50 per cent chance of causing death, but gives only a one-in-four chance of achieving the goal. It seems desirable that the law should provide him with an incentive for choosing the second course in addition to whatever disincentive it may provide from choosing either course.

In order to quantify his options in a simple way let us assume that the chances of detection are equal in either case – say fifty-fifty – and that he regards the punishment, if he is caught, as twice as great an evil as his goal is a good.

Now if the punishment for homicide does not distinguish between intentional and reckless killing then his rational course is to choose the more lethal option. If he does so and is caught, then he suffers an evil twice as great as the good he gains: he scores, let us say, minus 200 and plus 100, which leaves him with minus 100; if he is lucky and escapes, he scores plus 100; since the chances of escape and capture are equal these two prospects cancel out and provide no disincentive for the choice. On the other hand, if he chooses the less lethal option, then if he is caught he has an even chance of scoring minus 200, which gives this outcome the negative value of minus 100; its positive value is one quarter of 100, i.e. 25, so that the total value of this outcome is minus 75. The value of the other outcome of the option is plus 25, the one-in-four chance of achieving the goal worth 100. So the total value of the option, given thé equal probability of the outcomes, is minus 25. This makes it less attractive than the more lethal option.

If we now alter the penalties so that the punishment for intentional homicide is half as great again as that for reckless homicide (so that it has the value of minus 300) then we provide an incentive for him to choose the less lethal option. The value of the option remains minus 75; but the value of the more lethal option becomes minus 100 (since if he is caught the value of that outcome is now minus 200 instead of minus 100). If we simply increase the penalty for all homicide to minus 300 we would again provide him with no incentive to choose the less lethal option.

Of course, the assumption that the chances of detection are equal in either case is an unreal simplification. But if the simplification were removed the case for distinguishing intentional from reckless killing might be stronger. For it is often the case that the killing of a victim may reduce the chance of detection by removing a potential witness.

There is thus a case, simply on grounds of the efficient deterrence of harm, for making a distinction between reckless and intentional homicide and thus treating murder as a crime of specific intent. The justification of having crimes of specific intent in general is not difficult to see. Any law requiring specific intent as an ingredient of crime will prohibit one act A done with the intention of performing another B. Such a law has presumably as its purpose the prevention of the harm which is the result of B. It is necessary in cases where the prohibition of B by itself is thought insufficient protection against that harm. Other precautionary measures possible might be a simple prohibition on doing A, or a prohibition on doing any act with the intention of performing B. But either of these prohibitions may result in punishing more than is necessary – punishing cases of A with innocent intent (as we saw in Chapter 1 in the case of acts likely to assist a wartime enemy) and cases of acts done with the intention of performing B where there is no real chance of success and therefore of harm. Thus the economy of deterrence is best served by prohibiting the performance of A with the intent that B.

Thus we have seen the rationale, on the deterrent theory of punishment, for the discriminations made in law between the different forms of *mens rea* from negligence, recklessness and basic intent up to specific intent. It may well be thought that the theory behind such discriminations presupposes a coolness in calculation and a competence in the theory of games which it is unrealistic to impute to the average citizen tempted to commit a crime. On the other hand, it is surely not a mere accident that the gradations of severity in punishment which a comparatively recondite application of the theory of deterrence suggests should correspond in such large measure with the intuitions of moral common sense about the comparative wickedness of frames of mind.

In practice, of course, the deterrent effect of the law

operates unevenly and erratically. The elaborate efforts of lawyers and academics to sort offences into precise categories and to fit crimes to punishments on impeccable theoretical grounds may well strike a layman as resembling an attempt to make a town clock accurate to a millisecond in a community most of whom are too shortsighted to see the clockface, too deaf to hear the hours ring, and many of whom set no great store on punctuality in any case.

Those, on the other hand, who wish to abolish *mens rea* altogether in favour of strict liability and replace punishment with treatment misunderstand the nature of the social mechanism they are criticising as completely as one who should criticise a moderately efficient clock on the grounds that it was totally useless as a speedometer. The application of strict liability can be justified in special cases: particularly with regard to the conduct of a business. In such a case, even a strict liability statute makes an appeal to the practical reasoning of the citizens: in this case, when the decision is taken whether to enter the business and the strictness of the liability is a cost to be weighed. Strict liability is most in place when it is brought to bear on corporations. In such cases there may not be, in advance, any individual on whom an obligation of care rests which would ground a charge of negligence for the causing of the harm which the statute wishes to prevent: the effect of the legislation may be to lead corporations to take the decision to appoint a person with the task of finding out how to prevent the harm in question. But the justification of strict liability in such cases is a very different matter from the thoroughgoing abolition of *mens rea*.

In chapter 1 I tacitly assumed that when one distinguishes between *mens rea* and *actus reus* one could describe the *actus reus* without the use of mentalistic concepts. Except in a tiny minority of cases this is not so. For the great majority of human acts – buying, selling, giving information, threatening, promising, writing letters and a hundred others – are acts which can only be done voluntarily. A legal system which took no account of states of mind would be as chimeric as it would be abhorrent.

NOTES

1 Lord Macaulay, *Collected Works*, Longmans, London, 1898, vol. XI, p. 23.
2 The information in the present paragraph is taken from the summary of the evidence in Radzinowicz and King, *The Growth of Crime*, Hamish Hamilton, London, 1977, pp. 142–8.
3 In 'Mental Health in Plato's Republic', in A. Kenny, *The Anatomy of the Soul*, Blackwell, Oxford, 1973, pp. 25–6.
4 *Report of the Committee on Mentally Abnormal Offenders* (Butler Committee), Cmd 6244, 1975. ch 18.
5 Macaulay, *op. cit.*, pp. 110–15.
6 A. Woozley, 'Negligence and Ignorance or Mistake of Fact and of Law', to appear in a forthcoming issue of *Mind*.
7 I have discussed this question at greater length in 'Intention and Purpose in Law', *Essays in Legal Philosophy*, ed. X. Summers, Blackwell, Oxford, 1968; a paper which was illuminatingly controverted by H. Oberdiek in 'Intention and Foresight in Criminal Law', *Mind*, 1972, vol. LXII, pp. 389ff.

Appendix

While this book was in proof there appeared the Law Commission's *Report on the Mental Element in Crime* (HMSO, 1978). The Commissioners recommend that in all offences created after 1980 standard meanings should be given to terms denoting mental states; that it should be expressly stated to what extent liability in respect of a given offence depends on a particular mental state; and that in the absence of such express provision statutory presumptions should operate as to the type of fault which must be proved in order to secure conviction.

Because the Commissioners propose that their standard definitions and presumptions should apply only to offences to be created in future, the recommendations of the report do not directly affect anything said in this book about the current state of the law; but it is of interest to consider their proposals in the light of the analyses we have given of the concepts involved. The Report begins by illustrating in detail the uncertainties and ambiguities afflicting the current legal usage of terms such as 'malicious' 'wilful' 'with intent' 'knowledge' and 'recklessness': it makes a convincing case for replacing the present chaos with a limited vocabulary of mentalistic terms defined by standard tests. The terms for which it proposes statutory definitions, and which it hopes will be sufficient to cover the desired mental element in the great majority of cases, are 'intention', 'knowledge' and 'recklessness'.

While the proposal for standard tests is welcome, there appear to be defects in the formulation of some of the particular tests proposed; and the recommendation that terms other than the three listed should be avoided will reduce the flexibility at present enjoyed by the legislature (as illustrated in chapter 4 above).

The least satisfactory definition offered is that of intention. A majority of the Commission's preparatory working party on the topic had proposed the following definition: 'A person intends an event not only (a) when his purpose is to cause that event but also (b) when he has no substantial doubt that that event will result from his conduct'. The Commission disliked the word 'purpose' as suggesting 'motive', and instead proposes the following standard test of intention: 'Did the person whose conduct is in issue either intend to produce the result or have no substantial doubt that his conduct would produce it?' The use of the word 'intend' within the test will not help to clarify this confused area: as the Commission copiously illustrates in the first part of its report, there is no agreement at all among judges as to what the word 'intend' means, whether as a term of legal art or as an expression of ordinary language. Lords Dilhorne and Diplock are quoted on p. 7 of the report as construing 'intending a result' so broadly as to include 'foreseeing a result to be likely'. The Commissioners can hardly mean the word 'intend' in their test to be construed so broadly, because it would expand the area of intention so far as to be even broader than the area now proposed for recklessness. They indicate that they wish the word to be taken in its ordinary meaning: but they give little indication of what they take that ordinary meaning to be. Does 'intend' in its ordinary usage denote direct or oblique intention? That is, does it involve a desire to bring about a result, either for its own sake or in order to some further end; or will a merely cognitive state of knowledge or foresight suffice? The working party, however maladroitly, showed by its use of the word 'purpose' that it had direct intent in mind; the Commissioners leave the question wide open.

This ambiguity, it may be said, will not matter; if the word 'intend' in the first limb of the test means direct intention, none the less the second limb will ensure that oblique intention suffices for intent in law; whereas if 'intend' in the first limb means oblique intention, the second limb will at worst be superfluous, at best indicate the degree of certainty demanded for the foresight to amount to intention. But the most serious effect of the proposed definition of intention is that by lumping together direct and oblique it takes away from the legislature the possibility of requiring as the *mens rea* of a particular crime a direct intention, whether basic or specific. As was made clear above (p. 92) there can often be good reason for requiring direct intent, and as the law stands at present several crimes appear to do so. If the Commissioners' definition of 'intention' were accepted, and if it were again made an offence in wartime to do an act likely to assist the enemy with intent to assist the enemy, then someone could be guilty of an offence without in any way aiming to assist the enemy. If murder were to be defined as causing death with the intention of causing death or endangering life, then a surgeon who caused death by undertaking an operation known to be dangerous, or a person who accidentally took a life while driving a car dangerously in order to remove a time bomb from a populated area (see pp. 56–7 above) would be guilty of murder. There may be good reasons for urging the legislature to give up the possibility of requiring direct intent as an ingredient in *mens rea*: but the Law Commission offers no reasons for urging such a restriction in legislative practice, nor does it betray any clear consciousness that it is in fact being restrictive.

In the definitions both of 'intention' and of 'knowledge' the Law Commissioners make use of the notion of *substantial doubt*: a person 'is to be regarded as knowing that a particular circumstance exists if, but only if, either he actually knows or he has no substantial doubt that that circumstance exists'. We are given little indication how juries are to decide whether a doubt is substantial, beyond being told that the phrase will cover a person who deliberately shut his eyes to a fact which he claims not to know. One can foresee lengthy arguments about whether an accused's doubts were or were not substantial: but more serious is the question what the Commission means by 'doubt'. Is it a mental state? Is it possible to have doubts on a topic without ever thinking of that topic? If not, then a person who has never given a thought to the question whether the goods he has received are stolen will be free of doubt, substantial or otherwise, on the topic; he will therefore, by the Commission's definition, count as knowing that they are stolen.

In defining 'recklessness' the Commissioners have varied slightly the proposal of its working party already quoted on p. 63 above. The test of whether someone is reckless about the existence of circumstances is 'Did the person whose conduct is in issue realise that the circumstances might exist, and, if so, was it unreasonable for him to take the risk of their existence?' Like the working party definition this test, if applied to the construction of the word 'reckless' in the Sexual Offences (Amendment) Act 1976, would have the effect that a person with an honest but unreasonable belief that a woman was consenting to intercourse would not necessarily thereby be secure from conviction for rape if the woman did not in fact consent. For belief that p is compatible with realising that not-p might be the case (as the Commission recognises on p. 28 of its report); and so a man may honestly believe that a woman consents while realising that there is a risk that she does not and thus being 'reckless as to whether she consents'.

The Commission's proposals are based on a very thorough consideration of the present difficulty in construing the variety of mentalistic terms used in the law. It is to be hoped, however, that further consideration will lead to modification in the proposed tests before they become law. No doubt they will be the subject of considerable debate in and out of Parliament before being enacted. I hope that the present work may make some small contribution to the debate.

Index

Abbott, 36
Ability, 29–30, 41
Absolute liability, 61
Addiction, 43
Appetite, 27
Assault, 50, 64–6
Atkin Committee, 39
Authority, 74

Balance of justice, 71
Basic intent, 50
Beard, 65
Behaviourism, 10
Belief, 46
Bentham, Jeremy, 51
Black-out, 51
Bratty, 35
Butler Committee, 3, 41, 42,
    66–8, 81–4
Buxton, R., 68
Byrne, 41, 42

Cabin boy, 37–8
Capital punishment, 39, 43, 78–9
Careless driving, 8
Causation 22, 26–8
Chandler, 47–8
Choice, 26, 35
Churchill, W., 9
CIA agent, 60
Cognitive *v.* affective, 46, 51
Compartmentalisation, 44
Compatibilism, 25, 33
Compulsion, 35
Consent, 28, 51, 54

Consequences of actions, 47,
    50–1, 53
Covering laws, 21, 28
Criminal Justice Act 1967, 54
Criterion, 11
Cross of Chelsea, L. J., 55–6

Dangerous intoxication, 66–8
Debt, 72–3
Delaware, 79
Depraved heart, 52
Descartes, 10
Desmond, 53
Determinism, 9–10, 21–34
Deterrence, 75–8
Devlin, L. J., 47
Dilhorne, L. J., 55–6
Diminished responsibility, 40
Diplock, L. J., 55–6
Direct intent, 51–5
Drink, 64–6
Drugs, 64–6
Dualism, 10
Dudley and Stephens, 37
Duress, 35–9, 49–50

Economic determinism, 23
Elwyn-Jones, L. C., 65
Epilepsy, 65
Epistemology, 9, 11
Ethics, 10, 19
Euthanasia, 38

Fatalism, 23
Felony murder, 52

Fenians, 53
Foresight, 51–6
Forgery, 50
Freud, S., 23

Games theory, 90–2
God, 23

Hailsham, L. C., 55, 57, 59, 61
Hangover, 50
Hard determinism, 33
Heilbron Committee, 62
Homicide Act 1957, 40, 52
Hyam, 54–6, 61

Ifereonwe, 18
Incompatibilism, 33
Indifference, 25–6
Insanity, 39–44
Insurance, 8, 57
Intention, 6, 7, 36, 38, 48–63,
  90–3, 96–7
Intercourse, 57–63
Intoxication, 64–6
IRA, 36
Irresistible impulse, 39, 40–2

Jackson, 16–17
Justice, 70–3

Kenny, A., 54
Kilbrandon, L. J., 55
Killing, 14–15
Kitten-strangling, 31–2

Larsonneur, 35
Law Commission, 53, 63, 68,
  95–7
Libertarianism, 29
Liberty of indifference *v.*
  spontaneity, 25–6
Logical determinism, 23
Lufazema, 18–20
Lynch, 36

Macaulay, Lord, 78, 85–9, 91
M'Naghten Rules, 39–40, 80–4
Madness, 4–5, 39–43, 80–4
Majewski, 64
Malawi witchcraft statute, 18
Malice aforethought, 52
Manslaughter, 40, 67
Marx, K., 23
Mens rea, passim
Mental health, 4–5, 35, 39–43,
  80–4
Milk, 8
Mind, 10–12, 44
Mistake, 17
Model Penal Code, 41, 52
Morgan, 57–63
Motive, 48
Muabvi, 13–18
Murder, 36, 40, 52–6, 86

*National Association for Mental
  Health*, 3–8
Natural powers, 30
Nazi broadcasts, 49
Necessity, 36–8
Negligence, 85–8
Nyuzi, 12–21

Oberdiek, H., 94
Oblique intention, 51, 53–5
Official Secrets Act, 47
Omission, 85–8
Opportunity, 30
Ordeal, 12–15, 19

Palamba, 15–16
Parking offences, 5
Passport, 67
Payment, 71
Perjury, 8
Physiological determinism, 25,
  31
Practical reasoning, 80–3, 29
Prohibition, 77

Psychological determinism, 24–6, 32
Psychopaths, 81
Punishment, 69–93
Purpose, 21, 47–9

Radzinowicz, L., 94
Rape, 57–63, 98
Reasonableness of belief, 17, 58–63
Reasoning, 28, 44, 48, 80
Recklessness, 6, 60–3, 65–6, 88–90, 98
Referential opacity, 59–60, 68
Reflex action, 35
Remedial theories, 69, 74
Retribution, 69–73

Salmon, L. J., 36
Self-defence, 16–17
Sexual Offences (Amendment) Act, 62, 98

Simon, L. J., 38, 60, 62
Smith, 53–4
Soft determinism, 33
Special verdict, 32–4
Specific intent, 50, 52
Spontaneity, 25–6
Steane, 49–51

Theft, 49–50
Theological determinism, 23
Treason, 9
Treatment, 80–1

Vickers, 52, 55–6
Voluntariness, 24, 27, 34, 38, 42–3, 51, 64

Wanting, 27, 42
Will, 44
Witchcraft, 13–21
Wittgenstein, L., 11
Woozley, A., 88

DATE			
NOV 9 '84			
DEC 3 '86			
DEC 23 '87 DE 19 '94			
DE 31 '96 DE 18 '98			